250

Geraldine M. Bradley
Paris
June 1931

GOETHE AND BEETHOVEN

ROMAIN ROLLAND

GOETHE AND BEETHOVEN

Translated from the French by
G. A. PFISTER *and* E. S. KEMP

FULLY ILLUSTRATED

HARPER & BROTHERS PUBLISHERS
NEW YORK AND LONDON
1931

FIRST EDITION

B-F

CONTENTS

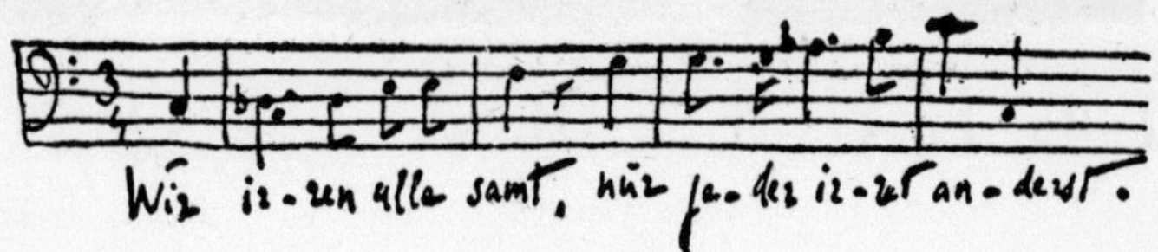
Wir ir-ren alle samt, nur je-der ir-ret an-derst.

ILLUSTRATIONS

LINE DRAWINGS IN THE TEXT

Translator's Prefatory Note

OF THE two giants, Goethe and Beethoven, who are the subject of this book, Beethoven is probably far better known to the English-speaking public than Goethe.

There are two reasons for this. Beethoven addresses the world in the language of music, a universal language, which can be understood by many who have not made even an elementary study of it. There is hardly a concert-goer in the world who has not heard Beethoven's symphonies or sonatas, or who has had no opportunity of feeling the influence of that mighty composer. The second reason is that there are many more people who, as amateur or professional musicians, have formed a closer acquaintance with Beethoven than that of mere hearing. They have played his works, analyzed them, interpreted them, and often enough, attracted by his work, have enquired into his life and his psychology. They have found at their disposal a comprehensive mass of literature, easily accessible; they have read of him in critical essays published in the press. And Ernest Newman's excellent translation of Romain Rolland's *Beethoven: the*

Creator has given those who read it, a deep insight into the composer's greatness.

Not so with Goethe. To understand and appreciate him is reserved to the comparatively small community which has a perfect knowledge of German, for no translation can do him justice. And those who do not know any of his works lack the interest which would prompt them to enquire into the great poet's life, thought, work, and influence.

Yet Goethe, the Olympian, as he is often called, was one of the greatest figures in literature which the world has known. He ranks with Homer, Virgil, Dante, and Shakespeare. Like these he belongs to the world rather than to a particular nation or race. He is, in literature, what Michelangelo and Raphael were in the realm of art, a sovereign master.

And, just as Michelangelo was supreme in every branch of his great art—painting, frescoes and architecture—so did Goethe excel in all that belongs to literature, from the short epigram, the sonnet, and the *Lied*, through the ballad and the descriptive poem to that mighty work *Faust* which has only one equal, Dante's *Divina Comedia.* For *Faust* is not only a poem of great beauty and a dramatic work of magnificent construction, but a deep psychological study of man and human nature. Goethe's dramatic works are equally great. From comedy, even farcical comedy, to great tragedies, such as, apart from himself, only Shakespeare has given to the world, he mastered every conceivable form. And in prose writing—romance, travel description, etc.—he was as great and as profound as he was in verse and drama.

Nor is that all. Goethe, who was not only a genius in literature, but a universal genius, perhaps the last of the few to whom this title may justly be given, was also a philosopher, a diplomat, a statesman, a scientist, an architect, and, as this book shows, a musician. And in all these realms he was a creator of the highest standard. His civil code, his works on colours, on botany (he was a forerunner of Darwin) made history. He was also more than an amateur in the art of painting.

In this respect, then, Goethe was more eminent than even Dante, who, like Leonardo da Vinci and Michelangelo, had mastered several branches of knowledge and art. And in this he surpassed Shakespeare, too.

Goethe's striking personality, both as a poet and as a man, could not fail to attract many women who, in their turn, inspired him to some of his finest work. Many of them—though by no means all—are mentioned in this book. They were of the most varying types: Friederike, the pastor of Sesenheim's charming child; Frau von Stein, the beautiful and highly intellectual aristocrat; and Christiana, the fat, red-faced, uneducated housekeeper, whom he finally married. The procession of women extended throughout his long life, from youth to old age, when, a widower of seventy-nine, he wanted to marry a girl of nineteen with whom he had fallen in love.

But among all these there was none upon whom Goethe had such a lasting influence, none whose influence upon Goethe was more durable, and none, perhaps, who understood the poet better than Bettina von Arnim-Brentano, the writer, musician, and champion of political freedom, the great dreamer and great lover.

If Bettina had a deep insight into Goethe's gigantic mind, she had an equally clear understanding of one who was his peer as no other, Beethoven. It was she who formed the link between these two, influencing the poet, championing the composer, appreciating both with a clairvoyance such as probably no other of their contemporaries has shown. To her also a great part of the present book is devoted.

Romain Rolland tells us of many occasions on which Goethe, after arduous planning and working, abandoned what he had set out to do. We read of failure, defeat, and wasted time and energy. This only shows that the great man's colossal work did not exhaust the still vaster possibilities of his creative mind. Fate was kind to him in many ways, but he had nevertheless a fair share of trials and disappointments. Had he been granted the fulfilment of all that he conceived and undertook, then indeed he would have been the king amongst supermen.

Romain Rolland's work, *Goethe and Beethoven*, will, it is hoped, be appreciated for the new light which it throws upon the relations of the two masters. It should prove also an inspiration to a wider and keener knowledge of two of the greatest men the world has ever known.

G. A. P.
E. S. K.

Note of Acknowledgment

The author and the publishers [illegible] thanks to all those who have assisted in the preparation of this volume. [illegible]

[illegible]

[illegible]

[illegible]

[illegible]

[illegible]

Note of Acknowledgments

The author and the publishers hereby extend thanks to all those who have assisted in the preparation of this volume. As in the case of *Beethoven: the Creator,* we have everywhere encountered the greatest spirit of cooperation, the most efficient aid.

We take pleasure in expressing our gratitude

To professor Max Hecker, Director of the Goethe and Schiller Archives of Weimar, who has given us permission to reproduce one of the three *Lieder* dedicated by Beethoven to Goethe;

To Professor Johannes Wolf, Director of the Prussian State Library of Berlin, who entrusted to us, for purposes of reproduction, two pages of the manuscript of *Egmont*;

To the Director of the Frankfurt Museum, from whom we obtained the little known portrait of Bettina as a girl.

We owe a special vote of thanks to Professor Anton Kippenberg, the eminent Director of the Insel-Verlag, who has more than once given us the benefit of his valuable advice and has allowed us to reproduce several items from his private collection, among them: the letter from Beethoven to Zelter, the views of Weimar, Teplitz and Marienbad which illustrate this volume, the portrait of Goethe by C. O. Kipinsky, the sketch of Goethe on his deathbed by Friedrich Preller, etc.

We are indebted also to Dr. Eugen Rentsch, Director of the Rotapfel-Verlag, and to Professor Max Friedlaender, the eminent historian and musicologist, who have shown a ready willingness to assist us.

To all of them our sincere thanks.

1

PRELUDE

I HAVE compared the writing of my book, *Beethoven: the Creator*, to a journey to the depths of Cyclops' smithy. When an old man like myself, who can count more than sixty years, embarks on travels as laborious as these, prudence suggests that he should not linger by the way, but make straight for the goal.

On the other hand, the journey's end never concerns me very much: it is the road which interests me if only it lie in the right direction. I never hurry. Poor creature that I am, existing since childhood's days under the ever-present threat of a life to be cut short, I have always lived as if a hundred years were my span—or as if I must die tomorrow. It matters little to me. The essential thing is the completion of the task to which my hand is set.

XVIII

On my Beethoven exploration, many a wayfarer has stopped me on the way; he has much to tell me and my ears are always open: I was born to be the confidant both of the living and of the dead. . . . Here are two whose lives were entwined with Beethoven's. One is Bettina, wild yet wise, a dreamer all her life; yet the eyes of the sleep-walker beheld Beethoven and Hölderlin, the men of genius whom their keenest contemporaries disowned. It was Bettina who foresaw the great revolutions. The other is Goethe, the teacher and comrade of every day of my life. In his works without number I have sought constant counsel since I was thirty years old, just as in the old days, when the shadows lengthened and the mind turned to its secrets, men used to open the family Bible. (You remember Faust, silent and meditative, in the twilight of his chamber.)

Goethe has never sent me away thirsty, or depressed me with long-dead principles. His were no abstract ideas, no *a priori* notions; he poured out a stream of lively and novel experiences, nature's spring, in which my youth was renewed. They are but few, even among the men of genius, whose souls commune unceasingly with the Spirit of the Earth, the *Erdgeist*. Goethe and Beethoven were two of the chosen of the Great Mother. But the one, he who was deaf, hearkened without understanding to the call from the depths, while the other beheld all, but heard part only. Bettina accompanies the two; intoxicated with dreamy visions and with love, she sees and hears nothing, groping for the path, stretching out her feverish fingers into the darkness.

To the readers of my *Beethoven* I offer this respite in my Odyssey upon what I have called that inner sea of Beethoven, begging them to rest awhile with me as Odysseus did in the land of Alcinous.

In these hurried times I love to breathe quietly as I lie outstretched in the valley of Villeneuve,* my hands clasped under my head, beneath the flowering cherry trees, on a day of the new-born spring. I gaze upon the vault of heaven and the changeless course of the centuries. . . . I recall talks in the Bohemian forest, Teplitz, the twin deities Goethe and Beethoven, and the love-lorn elegy of Bettina, "Nina, love's maddened victim."

Four essays compose this book. The first and the longest was once published in the review *Europa*; I have revised and completed it. The three others deal with the same subject, but present it from other points of view. Goethe's life was like an arrow shot from a

* *Translator's Note*—Romain Rolland's villa is at Villeneuve, Switzerland.

bow, which, once loosed, cannot be stayed in its flight to the ever receding target. The problem of that life is so vast even now, a hundred years after his death, and remains so fresh and vital, that truth, as I think, invites me to retain the freedom of presentment which I have displayed in these independent studies. In this way alone can I hope to follow the wonderful plasticity of the great model.

Music, I repeat, is the heroine of my story. I present her here not only as the companion of Beethoven-Dionysus, but as a Muse also; to Goethe, the Apollo of Weimar, she is not the least beloved of the Muses, a fact too little known. The main object of my book is to remind my hearers that the greatest poet of modern Europe belongs also to the fellowship of musicians. He is the river into which the twain converge, into which flow the twin streams of poetry and music, as do indeed all the streams of our Earth.

April 15th, 1930 ROMAIN ROLLAND

2

GOETHE AND BEETHOVEN

CHAPTER I

BEETHOVEN (ABOUT 1820)
DRAWING BY MARTIN TEJCEK

I

1811, 1812. . . . Autumn, the bountiful, with her vintage. The golden hues of the forest, the blazing sunset sky. The last days of love's autumnal splendour.[1] And the brief encounter of the two suns, Beethoven and Goethe. For centuries destiny had been shaping the converging course of these two planets of poetry and music. The meeting was soon over; the hour which had struck was quickly past. They met, they parted to follow each his course. Must we wait a thousand years yet for such another meeting? Happy were the eyes which beheld them. I look into these eyes to fathom the scenes that dwell there. In the bosom of the lake the reflection of parting day may yet be seen.

Though separated, they had long known each other.

But their knowledge was not equal; it was Beethoven who knew the other better.

From his earliest days he had steeped his mind in Goethe's works. He worshipped him,[2] he read Goethe every day. Goethe had taken the place which Klopstock had once filled in his heart.

"Klopstock always prays for death, and indeed he died soon enough, but Goethe lives and we must all live with him. That is why he is so easy to set to music. No writer may be set to music so readily."[3]

In his first conversation with Bettina in May, 1810, he had told her how much Goethe's poems fascinated him, "not only by their contents, but also by their rhythm. This language, composed after the noblest design, like an edifice erected by spirit hands, drives me, exalts me to write music. The secret of the harmonies is engrafted in it."

Bettina finds him aflame with the fire of inspiration which gave to the world two Goethe *Lieder*, and what *Lieder*! What music! *Trocknet nicht, Thränen!* ("Dry not, oh tears") and *Mignon.*

During the same year he wrote the music to *Egmont*, and since 1808 he had been thinking of setting *Faust* to music.

"To set to music" a poem was not for him, as for most composers, a labour of representation, a picturesque commentary on the words of the poem. It was a deep penetration of the verse, an intimate intermingling, as it were, of body and soul. It has not been sufficiently recognized that his words on the pursuit of melody, as reported by Bettina, refer actually to his attempts to fathom those of Goethe's thoughts which he desired to fuse with music.

"I must set myself therefore at the very focal point of enthusiasm; thence shall mighty discharges of melody flash forth far and near[5] (*Da muss ich denn von dem Brennpunkt der Begeisterung die Melodie nach allen Seiten ausladen*).

"Melody! I pursue her, I clasp her with new fire, she slips from me, is lost in the midst of vague impressions. Soon, driven by surging passions, I seize her again. I cannot loose myself from her, I must perpetuate her in a spasm of ecstasy with every urge of soul and body. And then, at the last, I triumph over her, I possess her whom I have pursued, for whom I have longed. And, behold—a symphony. . . . Yes, music is in very truth the mediator between the life of the senses and the life of the spirit (*Ja, Musik ist so recht die Vermittelung des geistigen Lebens zum Sinnlichen*). I long to talk of this to Goethe. Would he understand me?"

He declares "Melody is the sensual life of poetry (*Melodie ist das sinnliche Leben der Poesie*). Is it not through melody that the indwelling spirit of the poem permeates our being? Does not the melody of *Mignon* convey to us the whole sensual atmosphere (*Stimmung*) of the *Lied?*[6] And since our senses have responded to this impression, do they not react to it, are they not fired with a passion to continue their creative work?" . . .

Here Bettina attributes to Beethoven the intuition of a musical subconsciousness a thousand times deeper and vaster than the thought expressed by these words, stamping him thus as a forerunner of Schopenhauer and Wagner.

He turns again to Goethe, and his appeal becomes more insistent:

"Speak to Goethe of me; tell him that he must hear my symphonies! He will agree with me that music is the single, the immaterial entry into a higher world of knowledge which envelops man but which he cannot understand. . . . What the soul receives from music through the senses is spiritual revelation incarnate. . . . It is thus, if you understand me, that you must write of me to Goethe! . . . With all my heart I long for him to teach me."

But here, before resuming our way, we must stay a moment, and weigh the value of Bettina's testimony.

3

Although I cannot in this essay attempt to solve the enigma of this extraordinary woman, of whom I shall try to give a more detailed account elsewhere,[7] I must sketch for the reader an outline at least of the basic facts of the problem, and add the conclusions which I have reached.

We are now able to get a clear view of her mind. Some years ago her authentic correspondence with Goethe was published. Critical essayists have compared very carefully the wording of these letters.[8] In spite of gaps due to the disappearance of important letters, it is possible for us today, especially as to the period which concerns us, definitely to sift certainties from possibilities, possibilities from errors or inventions. The enigma of Bettina then no longer exists save for those who fail to understand the soul of women, or who lack the gift of that sympathy without which the doors of intelligence can never open.

No, she was in no way a "Sibyl of the North," as some of the modern historians have called the little Bettina Brentano of 1807 to 1810! When we describe a character, we must define clearly the period of which we speak; nothing remains constant during the course of a life time, least of all with a woman like Bettina, the slave of her own wild and tender heart.

Later, the features will alter, age will stamp them with many a wrinkle, and the youthful smile will lose its charm. And Goethe's eyes did not look upon her with the same favour in 1825 as they did in 1807.—But here we are concerned with the little Mignon, from her twentieth to her twenty-fifth year.[9]

A Mignon she appeared to her intimate friends, and to Goethe when they first met. And that is how she sees herself, as soon as she meets Mignon in *Wilhelm Meister.* She identifies herself with the character of Mignon, with her longing (*Sehnsucht*), her fate, "with everything," she says "except with her death"; for the demon of life possessed her.

She is small of stature, with a pale complexion, dark eyes like deep pools, and a mass of black curls.[10] Usually she wears a long trailing black dress, with a thick cord round her waist, like a pilgrim; she is independent of fashion and utterly unable to conform to the correctitude of polite society; she feels awkward on a chair, and is usually to be found crouching on a low stool, or perched in a window recess. She bubbles with life and laughter, or is lost in the deepest melancholy; she is fundamentally a great dreamer, to whom life is but a vision.

Young Alois Bihler, who drew this portrait of Bettina[11] at the moment when she was about to meet

Beethoven, could not sufficiently idolize and admire this charming girl—the riches of her mind, the bountiful spring of her fancy, her poetical passion, her natural grace, and the kindness of her heart. She was then twenty-five, but appeared to be only eighteen, or twenty at most; there was in her nothing false, nothing mean: she displayed a generosity without limit, of both mind and heart, and spontaneity without compare.

1810. . . . It is the year when Goethe, for long very reserved, is most in love with her, for he, too, has been unable to resist her charms.[12] It is the year, too, when she feels nearest to him and loves him utterly. Her whole existence is permeated with a passion for Goethe, dazzling and self-sufficing, a passion sealed with the mystical ring which, at their first meeting, he had been rash enough to put on her finger. Her letters of January and February, 1810, show that she was entirely absorbed in him, like the lovelorn Teresa of Avila. Nor must we think that Goethe wearied of this excessive adoration. He lapped it up, as a cat laps up sweetened milk. Not only does he thank Bettina for her love (February, 1810), but, having received no renewed protestations of affection for a whole month, he becomes uneasy and asks for them (May 10, 1810). He never parts with Bettina's letters; he takes them with him on his travels.

Now, it is in these circumstances that Bettina meets Beethoven for the first time. For what reason, unless at the call of an imperious sincerity, should she have written to Goethe that she had fallen in love with Beethoven and that he had vanquished her? Why else should she passionately have espoused Beethoven's cause, a course which—as she might well have known, and in fact did discover later on—was by no means to Goethe's liking.

Let me first continue the famous story which Bettina published years later.[13]

She had been staying for some time in Vienna with her brother, Franz Brentano, who had married Toni Birkenstock. The young couple were both faithful friends of Beethoven and kept up the noble traditions of art and learning of father-in-law Birkenstock, the friend of Franklin and Robertson. It was the month of May, a beautiful May, aflame with sunshine; Bettina's letters to Goethe are full of the splendour of gardens in flower, of the overpowering fragrance of the glass houses all open to the air.[14]

Bettina had heard one of Beethoven's sonatas which had overwhelmed her;[15] she longs to meet the composer. Everybody tries to dissuade her. Beethoven, they say, is unapproachable; no one even knows where he lives. Bettina, more than ever determined, takes the

4

risk. She finds the house; she enters.[16] He is seated at the piano and does not see her. She bends over him, whispering into his ear, "I am Betty Brentano." He turns round suddenly and sees this pretty girl with wide-open eyes which pierce his very thoughts; he notes her intense sympathy, her burning cheeks, when he sings to her *"Kennst du das Land,"* her throbbing soul, her fervent enthusiasm. How could he have resisted her?

She was equally captivated. In fact much more so than he.

> *"When I saw him, I forgot the whole world. When I remember our meeting, the world vanishes, . . . vanishes. . . . "*

She is so possessed by Beethoven that this giant, with his terrible loneliness, has become part of her; she shares the desert with him, and when the hot wind sears her she seeks refuge in the gentle affection and the fatherly tenderness of Goethe. Psycho-analysts should study the whole beginning of this letter to Goethe (in the *Briefwechsel* of 1835). It contains indeed a striking "mediumistic" phenomenon. Bettina's mind was one peculiarly susceptible to the electric[17] waves of other minds heavily charged with genius. The word *electricity* recurs often in her conversation with Beethoven.

Now she was fortunate in surprising Beethoven in the throes of a passionate crisis, in the grip of a creative trance, a "raptus," as he called it next day when she reminded him of what he had said.[18]

These conversations became the rule, for Beethoven, fascinated, would not let Bettina go, accompanied her to the Brentanos' house, took her for walks; Bettina, enraptured too, forgot everybody and everything but Beethoven— "Society, the picture galleries, the theatres, and even the spire of St. Stephen's Cathedral. . . ." Their discussions were on serious matters, a fact which later on Schindler doubted on the somewhat puerile ground that Beethoven had never mentioned it to him. But Schindler was not Bettina. When Beethoven, in his old age, addressed him, what he saw was the gloomy, obsequious face of his *famulus*, whose invariable complaint was, "It's raining."[19] *Famuli* do not inspire poets; they must be content with prose!

However, I am reserving the discussion of those of Beethoven's thoughts which Bettina reports, to another essay dealing more particularly with music. What concerns us here, in our history of the relations between Goethe and Beethoven, is whether the facts are true and Bettina's impressions sincere. There is no room for doubt either of the one or of the other. Apart from Bettina's letters to Goethe (in the *Briefwechsel* of 1835) and to Prince Hermann von Pückler-Muskau, the text of which can be questioned because they were published so much later, the letter to young Alois Bihler, of July 9, 1810, which is undoubtedly authentic, establishes the truth of her meeting with Beethoven and the shattering impressions which he made on her. He was extremely ugly, and this struck Bettina, who loved beauty above everything, more than any other woman; she could never really love Beethoven. Nevertheless, she was fascinated from the first moment, and remained so to the end—"*Ich habe diesen Mann unendlich lieb gewonnen*" ("I have become infinitely fond of this man").

What conquered her was the sublime greatness (*Herrlichkeit*), the unequalled sincerity (*Wahrheit*), of Beethoven, as expressed in his art. Moreover, she was attracted by his naïve attitude towards life, his complete defencelessness. The way in which people treated him revolted her. From that moment she devoted herself to his cause;[20] we shall see how loyally she defended him, even against those whose prejudices it would have been to her interest to overlook.

That she conquered Beethoven is equally certain. Her letter to Bihler tells us how assiduously Beethoven sought her company. During his last days in Vienna he never left her, he could not part from her, and when he had to go he begged her to write to him at least once a month, because he had no other friend.

Beethoven's authentic letter to Bettina, dated February 10, 1811,[21] tells us that she had written to him on two occasions and that Beethoven had carried these letters on his person during the whole summer, that he had been delighted with them, and that, in spirit, he had written her a thousand letters. He expresses his love, he sends kisses, and probably writes in much stronger terms than he would care to confess. That this man, immured from the world, living at that time in a state of artistic trance, blind, deaf, and insensible to all that was outside, intoxicated with the harmonies which filled his soul,[22] with the passionate communion which he held with the god within him, like one of the prophets of the Sistine*—that this damned-up torrent, suddenly finding an outlet, should have poured forth without restraint all the thoughts which were choking him, is in itself overwhelming evidence of his affection.

And now Bettina is to transmit to Goethe these thoughts of Beethoven. This point, too, is confirmed to us by evidence, although the circumstances were not quite as she told them.

* Translator's Note.—On the ceiling of the Sistine Chapel, Michelangelo painted his famous fresco showing the prophets of the Old Testament in the attitude of passionate oration.

When in 1834-35 Bettina published her *Briefwechsel*, she did not trouble about literal precision, and made no claim to it. After Goethe's death she had secured through Councillor von Müller the return of her letters written to the master. These she now published, but not in the disorder of style and thought of the originals.

She rewrote them and condensed several into one. And more, she completed them with her recollections of conversations she had had, using, perhaps, notes which she had made at the time, according to the custom of the day. We may be sure that she had often thought over her conversations with Beethoven, which, as we shall see, frequently puzzled her, and which she fully understood only many years later. She had no intention, in acting thus, to treat the truth lightly; on the contrary, she desired to express it more fully and more worthily on behalf of those whose memory she wished to serve. Having thus recast the letters, she gave them an approximate date, I might almost say a synthetic date, because one letter often covers correspondence and conversations extending over several months. The value to the historian of the *Briefwechsel* is in effect the value of Bettina's admitted powers of seeing, hearing, and understanding, powers which include a wise estimate as to how far it may be in her interest—she is quite unconscious of this—to speak the naked truth or to embellish it. This must be borne in mind as each letter is read. Whenever Goethe alone is the subject, it is advisable, no doubt, to remember Bettina's lovelorn tendency to idealize him, and to mingle her own life with that of her idol.

This, however, does not apply to Beethoven.

On the contrary, Bettina's worship of Goethe should have prompted her to neglect Beethoven, to avoid hurting Goethe, who, on this particular occasion, is of secondary importance to her. But she does nothing of the kind. Bettina battles bravely and passionately for Beethoven against everybody. Nothing in her whole life does her greater honour. It is only when we see her thus at close range that we discover the depth of her loyalty, in contrast with her superficial shortcomings, and appreciate the instinct of justice which in her is even stronger than the claims of love.[24]

In her *Briefwechsel* of 1835, Bettina publishes a letter which she is supposed to have written to Goethe on May 28, 1810, immediately after her first meetings with Beethoven, a letter glowing with the flame of his fiery words.

It is probable that she wrote down her thoughts every evening when she was alone after these memorable

5

meetings. For we see how, for months afterwards, she is troubled by them; they had caused a revolution in her mind. It is even possible that the rough notes of what had been said were shown to Beethoven, who, surprised when he read, in a quiet moment, the confidences uttered in an hour of abandon, is said to have exclaimed: "What? I said that? I? I must have been carried away!" But, in fact, the letter to Goethe was written only at the beginning of July, after Bettina had left Vienna and while she was enjoying, in her country home at Bukowan, a quiet time in which to recall the great memories of the month of May.

How deep and lasting had been the shock which Beethoven's advent had caused is shown by a little incident. In June, her brother Clemens came to join her with his friend, young Arnim. The latter, who felt sure that she returned his affection, found her distant and absorbed in thought. She told him that she meant to devote her life to the great cause of the time, to music (*"Hingeben zu grossen Zwecken der Zeit, an Musik"*). And when Arnim left, deeply distressed, and begged her in his letters to return his love, Bettina replied, affectionately and sincerely, that she would like to make him happy, but that she could not read clearly what was in her heart. Already in 1809 she had vaguely hinted to Arnim how fascinated she was by music (*"die Fesseln die mir die Musik anlegt"*). The meetings with Beethoven had strenghtened these bonds; opposing forces were at work within her.

On July 7th she began a long letter to Goethe, only to interrupt it twice; she continued it on the 13th, then on the 28th; she tried to pour into it the tide of feeling which had accumulated during the last three months. One feels that it obsessed her and that she could not free herself from her reflective mood.[25]

She put off time after time the moment when she was to utter what concerned her most. . . . At last she made up her mind, and began the account of her meeting with Beethoven. The words she used are the same as those which she employed at the opening of her imaginary letter published in 1835. In the latter she omitted some redundances. In the original letter she also insisted more on the common love for Goethe which had brought her closer to Beethoven. Her scheme is clear; in order to persuade Goethe to listen to her, she introduced Beethoven under the banner of Goethe. . . . Behold him! Bettina's heart is full to the brim; it is overflowing:

"And now, watch!" (*"Jetzt, giebt Acht!"*) I am going to tell you of Beethoven: (*"An diesem geht die ganze Welt auf und nieder wie . . ."*)[26] ("The whole world rises and falls around him, as . . .").

And with these mysterious words the letter abruptly ended; the sentence was left unfinished. Bettina could not continue. . . . It was impossible. . . . She had too much to say. . . .

Goethe, then at Karlsbad, wrote, on July 22nd, to his wife that he had received a short note from Bettina, without date or address, informing him that she would either come to Weimar in the near future or write him a long letter. Bettina, who had felt how very difficult it was to express in writing to Goethe the overwhelming emotion which the discovery of Beethoven had roused in her, and who, no doubt, had written more than one letter, only to destroy it again, left her confession to the next meeting. It would be easier to speak than to write it.

This meeting took place sooner than either Bettina or Goethe expected. It so happened that while Goethe was summoned to Teplitz by his grand duke, Bettina, on her way to Berlin by way of Prague, passed through Teplitz, heard that Goethe was there, and hurried to meet him. In two days, two beautiful days of happy intimacy, August 10 and 11, 1810, she poured out at last in full flood the revelation which had enriched her life, which had shaken it to the depths.

"She has talked to me endlessly," writes Goethe, "of

her adventures old and new" (*"Sie hat mir unendliches erzählt von alten und neuen Abenteuern"*).

The new adventures were her meeting with Beethoven. Goethe avoids mentioning his name; he refuses to attach importance to Bettina's enthusiasm. What was his opinion of Beethoven? He thought very little of him at that time,[27] and, as we shall see, not much good, either. But at that moment he was too much taken with the charms of the pretty girl to stop her flow of narrative. He was watching her lips, without listening to the words.

"Bettina was really prettier and more charming than ever" (*"Bettina war wirklich hübscher und liebenswürdiger wie sonst"*). So he writes very foolishly the day after her departure, to his jealous Christiana, who never forgot it.

He was not listening, and yet he heard. . . . What was Bettina saying?

She was telling him what she wrote later on in her imaginary letter of 1835. This was not an exact account of her first visit to Beethoven, but of all her visits combined, all the days they spent together, all the walks, the reflections, and the overwhelming impression made on her by this great man; distance lent him an added stature in her mind and vivid recollections crowned him, as it were, with a halo.

I have no reason whatever to doubt the material accuracy and the moral certainty of her impressions, though the words which she attributed to Beethoven in her version of 1835 are probably not literally reported.

Bettina's burning imagination has probably gilded the picture, and the artistic gifts natural to her were no doubt responsible for its composition. But her picture of Beethoven is as true as that famous painting by Claude Lorrain of the Roman Campagna. Scrupulous realism could not reproduce more faithfully the plains of Rome and the brilliance of the light. Thus with the Beethoven whom Bettina saw and painted. No other eye has fathomed the depth of his genius so deeply as hers; feminine intuition absorbed his secret thoughts even before Beethoven himself had a clear conception of them.[28] It is a plunge into the fiery furnace of the Cyclops. Bettina listened, just as Beethoven spoke, in a *raptus*, and that is why she perceived what ponderous intellectuals, who know nothing of the lightning which illumines the soul, are unable to grasp.

Goethe, however, knew this lightning and did not appreciate it, he realized its danger, and preferred a horizon free from it. What, then, did Goethe think? Interested, but rather at a loss, he refused to take very seriously what he called later on Bettina's *"Wunderliche Grillen"* ("Strange whims").[29] But his ever alert psychological curiosity was at the same time attracted and repulsed, by these "problematical characteristics, all the more so because they are so difficult to define and to decipher."[30] He was struck by the extraordinary figure conjured up by Bettina; later we shall see this from the haste, so unusual in him, with which he went to see Beethoven at Teplitz. Goethe probably never wrote, and for good reasons, the letter of June 6th, which Bettina attributes to him,[31] and which would have been written soon after she left. It must be added that, not content with their long conversations, she left with him a lengthy written account, and sent him, three days later, yet another letter, even more ardent than those which preceded it. Goethe replied on August 17th, expressing both the surprise and the joy which he derived from these pages which she had given him and which he read over and over again. "And now comes your last letter which surpasses all the others. . . ." Never before had Bettina made a stronger impression upon Goethe.[32] Never before had he formed a higher conception of her mental capacity; and as, in his genial egoism, he was apt to judge other people by the value of the spiritual booty which they brought him, he immediately bore witness to the high esteem which he had

6

conceived for her, by associating her with his own work.

At that time, then, Beethoven would have been very near to forcing an entrance into Goethe's intellectual sympathy, had not a third person been present at these conversations who counteracted Bettina's efforts, Zelter.

We know of the solid friendship which bound Goethe to this clumsy artisan of music, this good fellow, sound musician, perfect Philistine, and faithful Achates to his Æneas. No other bonds proved more durable than this friendship. It has its noble side; but a deplorable law governing genius seems to decree that, with the superior mind, a strong dose of mediocrity in the other is required to satisfy the needs of friendship. A genius will form only a passing friendship with his peers. After Schiller's death the circle in which Goethe lived was, almost without exception, astonishingly barren; it comprised provincial bourgeois twenty years behind their time, dense, narrow, and warped. Young people who called on him were often scandalized at this. In his band of workmen, whose devotion was unshakable, Zelter was, and remained to the end, the foreman, the sole oracle on the subject of music. It was on his sincere and obtuse lack of understanding that Goethe passively relied in deciding what to admire and what to reject.

What then, did his Zelter tell him of Beethoven?[34]

November 12, 1808. . . . "With admiration and awe we behold will-o'-the-wisps on the horizon of Parnassus, talents of the greatest significance, like Beethoven's, using the club of Hercules to kill flies. At first we are surprised, then we shrug our shoulders at the sight of this display of talent, employed to invest trivial things with importance."

A little later[35] he became more virulent. Speaking of Beethoven's works, he was not content to refer to them as monsters "whose father might be a woman, or whose mother might be a man"; he suspected them of being immoral. *Christ on the Mount of Olives,* which, no doubt, is not a great work, but which certainly does not deserve this clamour of outraged modesty, he considered to be "an unclean work (*Unkeuschheit*) the reason and the end of which is everlasting death. I know," he continues, "music-lovers who used to show alarm, or even indignation, on hearing these works; now, however, they are roused by them to an enthusiasm which is akin to that of the devotees of Greek sexual perversion. . . ." (*"Wie die Anhänger der griechischen Liebe"*).

The art of the chaste and virile Beethoven accused of immodesty and sexual perversion! It might be called a malevolent and foolish joke! It would be laughable, if we did not remember into whose ears this poison was poured, though by a hand which we must admit to be without malice, as Zelter himself proved later. . . . "Unbalanced, monstrous, immodest, perverted Art:" in ten lines Zelter found everything which could erect an everlasting barrier between Goethe and Beethoven.

Bettina, then, met Zelter at Goethe's house on the evening of August 11, 1810, at Teplitz. We can imagine the unkind remarks, the scoffing, the clumsy arguments, the rough-and-ready words with which Zelter commented on the mystic-musical flights of Bettina. The little cat arched her back and spat at the growling cur from Berlin. Goethe, in a short note of August 13th in which he praised Bettina's charm, says: "But towards other people she is very rude" (*"Aber gegen andere Menschen sehr unartig"*).

When Bettina left Teplitz she took with her a solid hatred of Zelter. She ruminated over it the whole winter. In this, again, she showed her loyalty. She knew perfectly well that it was dangerous to attack Zelter's influence on Goethe, that it was labour lost, and that she risked the forfeiture of her idol's good will. Nevertheless, she refused to forgive this "Philistine," as she called him, his gross and malevolent lack of understanding of Beethoven. When she met him again in Berlin, where poor Arnim was ill advised enough to recommend Zelter to her as a teacher of harmony, and was snubbed for it, her letters to Goethe were filled with sarcastic references to the clumsy pedant "whose bones are so large and whose waistcoat is so long" (*"mit so breiten Knochen, und so langer Weste"*). She puts them all into the same bag, these Berlin pedants—Zelter, Reichardt, Rigini, and Himmel; they were always quarrelling, always barking at one another and at the passers-by. Let them bite and bludgeon one another, but the great men, the glorious dead and Beethoven, must be left in peace.[36]

Goethe frowned. He had hoped that these musical fancies would be forgotten, like the whims of a pretty woman. When he found that they were an obsession he was annoyed. At first he was guarded, for he had need of Bettina. For the memoirs which he intended to write he must draw on recollections of his boyhood, and Bettina had gathered the details from the lips of his mother during the days which the two women spent together, hours of delight in which they pictured once again the sunrise of the young god. Goethe himself, strange to say, remembered nothing of his youth; his Frankfurt days were dead. Without the help of her who had been his mother's youthful confidante, he could not have described a single incident of his earlier years. Thus he had to extract from Bettina those treas-

IIte. Ansicht der Stadt Töplitz in Böhme

II

IInd Vüe de la ville de TÖPLITZ en Bohême.

...av.

ures which she had gathered for her own delight. Drop by drop she distilled them for him, interpolating unkind remarks about Zelter, and introducing the nebulous theories of her fevered brain on "music-revelation" and the genius of Beethoven, fancies which are illumined at times by a lightning flash of inspiration.[37] Goethe had to accept all she gave him. His bad temper was only revealed by his silence, but his resentment grew. Some words in his letter of January 11, 1811, show it:

"On many occasions you are as stubborn as a mule and especially when you speak of music. In your little silly head you concoct some extraordinary fancies; however, I am not going to lecture you or cause you any pain."

In other words, "You can talk as long as you like; I shall not honour you by a discussion."

During this winter of 1810-11 Goethe broke with Bettina. He thought he was the only lord and master of this fascinating mind, the dual nature of which, Italian and German-Rhenish (she was the daughter of his early-beloved Maximiliana La Roche), attracted him. She had come to him, and it seemed as if she were his. Now, while reassuring the god of Weimar of her admiration, she parted company with him in order to follow the new revelation which had come to her from Beethoven and to identify herself with the young romantic movement in Germany!

After long hesitation, Bettina became engaged to Arnim (December 4, 1810) and married him in the following spring (March 11th). The letter in which she informed Goethe of this event, and which was written two months later (May 11th), is really devoted more to Goethe than to Arnim; no doubt her sincere affection for Arnim was a very pale flame compared with her passion for Goethe, which lasted all her life. But, unconsciously, Goethe thought himself betrayed, and smarted under the disappointment. The wound was above all intellectual. Achim von Arnim, a young gentleman of letters, was worthy of the highest esteem both for his talent and for his character; he showed for Goethe much respect and consideration, which the elder man appreciated; but in the domain of the intellect Arnim, like Beethoven, with due regard to the difference between the two, was the enemy. I am wrong, he was not; it is Goethe who was Arnim's enemy. The tide of neo-romanticism which was rising round him troubled and exasperated him. He believed that the whole edifice of his life was threatened with destruction. And though the new generation asked nothing better than to kneel before him, and receive the accolade of chivalry, he could scarcely hide from them his animosity. It broke forth with unrestrained violence in a letter written in October, 1810, the object of which was, as a matter of fact, the noble-minded and innocent Arnim.

"There are moments," Goethe writes, "when they drive me to distraction. I have to control myself so as not to be rude to Arnim, who sent me his *Countess Dolores*, which I like well. If I had a son gone astray, I would rather know that he had wandered into brothels, and even into pigsties, than that he should lose himself in the bedlam of the present day, for I fear that from this hell there is no salvation."[39]

What do those who always see in Goethe an Olympic figure think of this flow of brutal temper? If we wish to understand his aversion for his time, let us think of our own days, of the present crisis in European art, uprooted today as then by a World War and by social upheavals; let us note the confusion of faked folly, faked reasoning, faked religion, faked poetry; let us consider the degradation of the mind which swings frantically like a pendulum from anarchy to serfdom, from the excesses of liberty to the excesses of tyranny! An epoch which, perhaps, in spite of its basic incoherence and destructive fury, may be pregnant with greatness, a necessary transition from a dying world to a world yet to be born. . . . But a man like Goethe, who knew what it had cost him to establish order in his art and in his life, could not see all that he had won in imminent danger or ruined, without a feeling of disgust. This sentiment was all the stronger because of his keen insight into the dangers which beset the German mentality with its chronic lack of balance. He had felt, too, very deeply the disgrace to which these excesses inevitably lead.

To preserve, in the face of these revolutions, the ironic impassivity of a Renan, Goethe would have had to be a Renan himself, a man who essayed everything, but retained nothing. Goethe, however, was Goethe, and what he had he held; he left nothing to the changes and chances of life. A man of peace, he was always armed.

He is often compared to Phœbus Apollo, a romantic aspect of him immortalized in the fine bust by Martin Gottlob Klauer, the sculptor; there are certain traits in the life and character of the god which he exhibits in a marked degree. He shows us the god in exile; the god in solitude; the god who fights the dragon but who is too proud to proclaim his struggles and the dangers he has faced; the god who fights alone and who alone, as day succeeds day, ascends the path which leads to the great light.

He was Goethe, the man who rarely laughed, who

8

9

10

11

took life and art seriously, slow to forgive those who, in the lightness of their hearts, would trouble his sense of order and of harmony.

If, then, the inoffensive Arnim caused him to empty the vials of his wrath, what of Beethoven?

Goethe was not enough of a musician to see in Beethoven what we in our day perceive at once and what Bettina had so cleverly divined, the sovereign mastery (*Herrlichkeit*) of his will in matters of art, over the unfettered elements. He was, however, musician enough, as was Tolstoi, to perceive the unchaining of these elements, and to be frightened by it. The rushing of the flood was in his ears, but not the *quos ego* of deliverance. Beethoven's dominance of the elements, even had he realized it, would not perhaps have reassured him on his own account. Let us say plainly that, on the edge of *any* abyss, Goethe felt giddy. He considered Beethoven, gesticulating on the verge, as a lunatic, a sleep-walker who, sooner or later, would topple into the depths. He repulsed the hand of the madman outstretched to clutch him. . . .

I had written these lines before reading the scene which now follows: it will show that my intuition was correct.

On the 12th of April, 1811, Beethoven wrote to Goethe.[40] His letter, touchingly modest, overflowed with affection and respect. He told Goethe that he would send him shortly the music to *Egmont*,[41] and asked for his opinion:

"Yes, even adverse criticism will benefit me and my art; I shall be as pleased to receive it as the highest praise."

It is worth noting that this humble great man, humble only with Goethe, proud towards all others, had already sent to Goethe through Bettina, in the course of the previous year, three admirable *Lieder* to words by Goethe, and that the latter had made no reply. Yet Beethoven, when he wrote again, uttered not a syllable of impatience or a hint of reproach. He repeated the offering with the same humility.

The letter was brought to Weimar by Beethoven's secretary, Franz Oliva, a distinguished and likable young man, of whom Varnhagen and Rahel have spoken with much esteem. Goethe invited him to dinner on May 4, 1811. After the meal, Oliva sat down at the piano and played Beethoven. What did Goethe do?

While Oliva was playing, he walked impatiently up and down the music-room with Boisserée. The latter, who did not like Beethoven's works, either, amused himself by looking at Runge's paintings hanging on the walls, paintings which were indeed by a great artist whose charm and originality have recently won renewed recognition. Goethe, much vexed, said to Boisserée:

"What! You do not know that? Well, just look at it! It is enough to make one mad (*Zum Rasendwerden*)! Beautiful and crazy, at the same time!" . . .

"Yes, just like Beethoven's music which that fellow over there is playing (*der da spielt*)." . . .

"Exactly," growls Goethe. " 'That' wants to grasp everything, and 'that' always loses itself in elementary things, and yet some details are infinitely beautiful.[42] . . . Look!"—and here we do not know whether he was speaking of Runge or Beethoven, because the deprecating judgment included both—"What devilish work (*Was für Teufelszeug*)! . . . And here, again, what charm (*Anmuth*) and splendour (*Herrlichkeit*) this fellow (*Kerl*) has produced! But the poor devil could not keep it up, he is done with already (*er ist schon hin*). It was bound to happen. People who stand on seesaws[43] either perish or go crazy (*verrückt*); for that there is no pardon (*da ist keine Gnade*)." . . .

For a few moments he remained silent. Then followed a fresh explosion:

"You can hardly understand! For us old men it is maddening (*Toll werden*) to have to see all around us a decaying world, a world returning to its elements until—God knows when—things will change for the better!" . . .

It would be difficult to disclose more effectively the innermost secret of his thought, the hidden tragedy. This subtle malevolence for Beethoven was really his vital instinct on the defence, the hatred of one who feels that what he holds dearest is threatened.

However, he was a man of the world and knew what good manners demand, what was due to the advances of a distinguished composer who had shown him such great respect, what was due also to the insistence of Bettina, who in her letter of May 11th[44] pleaded Beethoven's cause with such warmth. So on June 25th he at last replied with a cordial politeness from Karlsbad.[45] He did justice to Bettina, and pointed out to Beethoven the value of such an advocate:

"Bettina fully deserves the sympathy which you have shown the dear girl. She speaks of you with the greatest admiration and affection. She counts the hours she spent with you among the happiest of her life."

He will be glad, he continues, to find on his return the promised *Egmont* score, and he thinks that he will be able to have it played at the performances of this drama the following winter. "Thus I hope to give great enjoyment both to myself and to your numerous admirers in our country." He hoped that Beethoven

Nach d. Nat. gez. v. Basili Hacker — Grav. v. Prof. C. A. Richter.

MARIENBAD IN BÖHMEN

II[te] Ansicht.

C G Hammer sc.

Der Kreutzbrunnen zu Marienbad. | La source dite Kreutzbrunnen à Marienbad.

would come to see him, as Oliva promised, and advised him to choose the season when the court and the musical public would be in town.

"You are sure to find in Weimar a reception worthy of your great merits. . . . But no one could be more interested in your visit than I, who beg to express my most cordial thanks for all the kindness which you have shown me."

The letter was written then in as affectionate a tone as Goethe could use towards a musician whom he knew only by hearsay,[46] and whose art had no great attraction for him. It seems to me that this was indeed a great triumph for Bettina.

When, at the end of January, 1812, he at last received the music to *Egmont*, he had it played to him on the piano by an amateur, Friedrich von Boyneburg,[47] several times in the course of the same day. From this it would appear that he was making an effort to understand Beethoven; the hope seemed justified that, in spite of all that separated them, the two men would join hands in friendly alliance.

But just at that moment a catastrophe occurred. Beethoven lost his little patroness at Weimar. During the summer of 1811 Goethe suddenly broke off his relations with Bettina. The Arnims were shown the door.

And at that fatal hour an evil chance brought Goethe and Beethoven face to face.

GOETHE AND BEETHOVEN

CHAPTER II

BEETHOVEN (1823)
DRAWING BY VON LIFER

14

II

GOETHE'S break with Bettina in September, 1811, was like a thunderclap out of a cloudless sky. But the storm had been gathering for a whole year, since Bettina's visit to Beethoven, and the rebellious enthusiasm which she consequently displayed.

The newly-wedded Arnims had come to Weimar for their honeymoon. At first everything went smoothly. They were to have stayed for a week, and Christiana's jealousy was smoothed by her assumption that "Bedina,"[48] now happily married, was no longer dangerous. The young couple were affectionately received; they were at Goethe's house morning, noon, and night; they never left him. The first week's stay was followed by a second, then by a third. The state of Bettina's health justified, it is true, the extension of their visit, but not in the eyes of Goethe, with whose work it interfered, nor in those of the *Frau Geheimrat* ("Mrs. Privy Councillor"), who, to her bitter disappointment, soon discovered that Bettina's marriage made no difference in her spiritual flirtation with the *Geheimrat*.[49] The two women were certainly not born to understand, or even to tolerate, one another; the worthy fat Christiana, so simple and so vulgar (with age and good living she became redder and fatter, more and more vulgar), and Bettina, delicate and difficult, with her sentimental fancies and her never-ending "ideas." Both had ready, lively and uncompromising tongues: both were up in arms in the presence of the man whom both, for different reasons, considered their property. They met every day, smiled at each other, and kissed . . . they would much rather have bitten each other! The Arnims, like everyone else in Weimar society, sympathized discreetly with the hen-pecked great man. Christiana, on the other hand, incited Goethe against the guests who took advantage of him. The storm broke suddenly while the two women were visiting a picture-gallery, and a real tornado it was. Bettina knew something of art and exercised her wit at the expense of the daubs which were shown. The organizer of the exhibition was the *Hofrat* Heinrich Meyer, an old friend of Goethe's family, whose taste, like that of Zelter and all the old *habitués* of the house, was somewhat mildewed. Christiana, therefore, took the offence as a personal affront; unable to meet Bettina, who excelled in ironical humour, on her own ground, the apoplectic lady gave vent to her accumulated wrath in screams and gesticulations. Bettina was accustomed to adorn her impudent little nose with a lorgnette or with glasses; they were torn from her, thrown to the ground and smashed. In the hearing of a curious crowd, attracted by her cries, the offended wife forbade her rival, who was struck dumb with surprise, ever to set foot again in their house. It was a public scandal. The whole town eagerly supported Bettina. So good an opportunity of attacking Christiana and Goethe could not be missed, for the bourgeois morality of Weimar had never forgiven their scandalous marriage. Goethe had necessarily to take sides with his wife, and closed his door to the Arnims.[50]

At heart, he did not regret it. Their departure meant the end of a romantic folly. Henceforth he would have peace, peace in the company of Zelter, Riemer, Meyer, and others like them, peace and the old order of things. Arnim, writing to Grimm at the end of September, said:

"You can hardly imagine the incredible surroundings in which he lives, separated from the rest of society by his wife. And how he fears everything novel in art, everything which is not well ordered (*Unordnung*). It is almost laughable. He will say of anything new: "Yes, it is a very good joke (*recht gute Spässe*), but I am no longer interested. (*aber sie gehen mich nicht mehr an*). It almost seems as if the writing of his biography (at which he had been working for a year) has suddenly aged him, and his way of thinking."

But the astounding adaptability of Goethe's genius enabled him to recapture the spirit of his lost youth; we find in the *Westöstlicher Divan* a springtime of exuberant passion, and a dazzling flight of fancy in the last *Faust* and the immortal song of the watcher, Lynceus, whose "happy eyes" are ever open.[51]

But a period of sheer despondency and hopelessness preceded each of these revivals.

He who knew himself so well needed complete isolation in such moments. And, indeed, he found this isolation, and enjoyed it to the full, in the honest mediocrity of his faithful *famuli*, and in his good wife's absence of intellect; a housewife all smiles, bright, clean, but how vulgar! Nevertheless, this comfort and sense of ease were dearly bought. Those who persist in seeing in him "the supreme artist of life" are quite unaware of the hidden misery of his domestic life; they have no idea of all the compromises and the af-

Wöchentliche Beschäftigung.

Montag den 23sten Septbr: 1816

früh um 10. Uhr Probe;
Am Abend die Vorstellung von
Nathan.

Dinstag den 24ten ej:

früh um 10. Uhr Clavierprobe
von Griselda.
Nachmittag ganze Probe von Fidelio.

Mittwoch den 25ten ej:

die Aufführung der Oper: Fidelio.

Donnerstag den 26ten ej:

früh um 10. Uhr Vorprobe von;
Welches ist der Bräutigam.
Nachmittag um 4. Uhr Clavierprobe
von Griselda.

Freitag den 27sten ej:

früh um 10. Uhr Hauptprobe von
Welches ist der Bräutigam.
Nachmittag um 4. Uhr Clavierprobe
von Griselda.

Sonnabend den 28ten ej:

die Vorstellung des Lustspiels.
Welches ist der Bräutigam.

Die andere Woche Sonnabend
den 5ten Octbr: dürfte die Oper
Griselda die Reihe treffen.
Sign: Weimar d. 19ten Septbr: 1816.
Großherzogl: S. Hoftheater Intendanz

Goethe

fronts which he must endure, of the bitter thoughts which he must hide, and, when things become unbearable, of his flights from home, lasting often for months. . . . No, he was a "supreme artist" only in his art; his life, seen at close range, inspires us not so much with admiration as with pity.[52]

So Bettina, in spite of her regrets, her constant love, and her efforts to make peace with Goethe and to forget the quarrel, was exiled from the circle of friends in Weimar. For six long years all correspondence ceased between her and her idol.[53] Even when they began to write to each other again, Bettina never recaptured the good graces of the sorely vexed "Olympian." Beethoven no longer had an advocate to plead his cause with Goethe.

And just at that moment the two were to meet; fate unexpectedly decreed that they should come together.

In July, 1812, while Goethe was at Karlsbad, he received a letter from his grand duke asking him to come at once to Teplitz, where the young Empress of Austria[54] wished to meet him. Goethe went to Teplitz; Beethoven had already been there for a week. It was not to see him that Goethe went there, but, being in the same town, he remembered, no doubt, the striking picture which Bettina had drawn of Beethoven, and the latter's ardent desire to meet him. His mind misgave him, but the inquisitive eagerness of the expert in human character won the day.

Teplitz was then full of emperors and empresses, gorgeous archdukes and court ladies.[55] Beethoven, however, was not one of those who were impressed by their dazzling plumage. He wrote in his grumbling way: "There are few men, and among those few, none of outstanding merit; I am alone, quite alone."[56]

It was then that he wrote to a little eight-year-old girl the exquisite letter in which we find the famous passage: "I can admit no other sign of superiority than a good heart."[57]

On the same day, in a letter to his publishers, he suddenly exclaims, in the midst of business matters, "Goethe is here."[58]

We feel how stirred he was by his presence.

Goethe acted in noble fashion. He was the first to call (Sunday, July 19th). And he, too, like Bettina and so many others was conquered at first sight. On the same day he wrote to his wife:

"Zusammengefasster,[59] energischer, inniger, habe ich noch keinen Künstler gesehen" ("Never before have I met an artist of more powerful concentration, more energy or deeper sincerity").[60]

This is saying a great deal. During his whole life Goethe had never honoured any other man by such a testimony of superiority.

How wonderful was his insight, how torrential his energy, how superhuman his power of concentration, how fathomless the depth of his inmost feeling! Goethe, surveying the world of men, sees more freely, more accurately, more deeply than he understands; in one piercing glance he has grasped the essentials in Beethoven's genius and unique personality.

That Goethe was greatly impressed is shown by the fact that the next day, July 20th, they went out walking together. On the day after, the 21st, Goethe went to see Beethoven, in the evening. He called again on Thursday, the 23rd, and Beethoven played to him at the piano.

Four days later, on the 27th, Beethoven left Teplitz for Karlsbad, where his medical adviser had sent him; Goethe was only there from the 8th to the 11th of September. Did they meet? We do not know. On the 12th Beethoven left Karlsbad again for Teplitz, to which Goethe did not return. It was the end. During their whole life the two men were never to meet again.

What had happened? A generous impulse had drawn them together. The first few days revealed an undeniable attraction. . . . And then, silence.

We find a clue in two letters connected with Bettina. Their authenticity has been questioned,[61] but in my opinion this truth is proved by circumstances which I shall describe later, and by two other letters, unfortunately only too authentic, one from Beethoven to Breitkopf (August 9, 1812), and the other from Goethe to Zelter (September 9, 1812)—not to mention the gossip then current in Teplitz, which in itself is eloquent enough.

I shall try to look on these two men, and to describe them, as they were, with all their greatness and their pettiness. Defects are to be found even more in men of genius than in ordinary men: both Beethoven and Goethe had a full share of them.

At first, as I have said, Goethe was the more generous of the two. He held out his hand to Beethoven. He was as cordial as he could well be, considering that he was naturally inclined to stiffness, except in his art and with his bosom friends. Beethoven did not disappoint him, nor did the next day's impression contradict the first. But Beethoven seems to have been less favourably impressed by Goethe. The poet, of whom he had dreamed since childhood, whom he had likened to an eagle flying with mighty wings in the teeth of the blast, proved to be a *Geheimrat*, much concerned with etiquette, and profoundly respectful of rank; he was a

[illegible]

leidvoll [illegible]

Hangen und

[illegible]

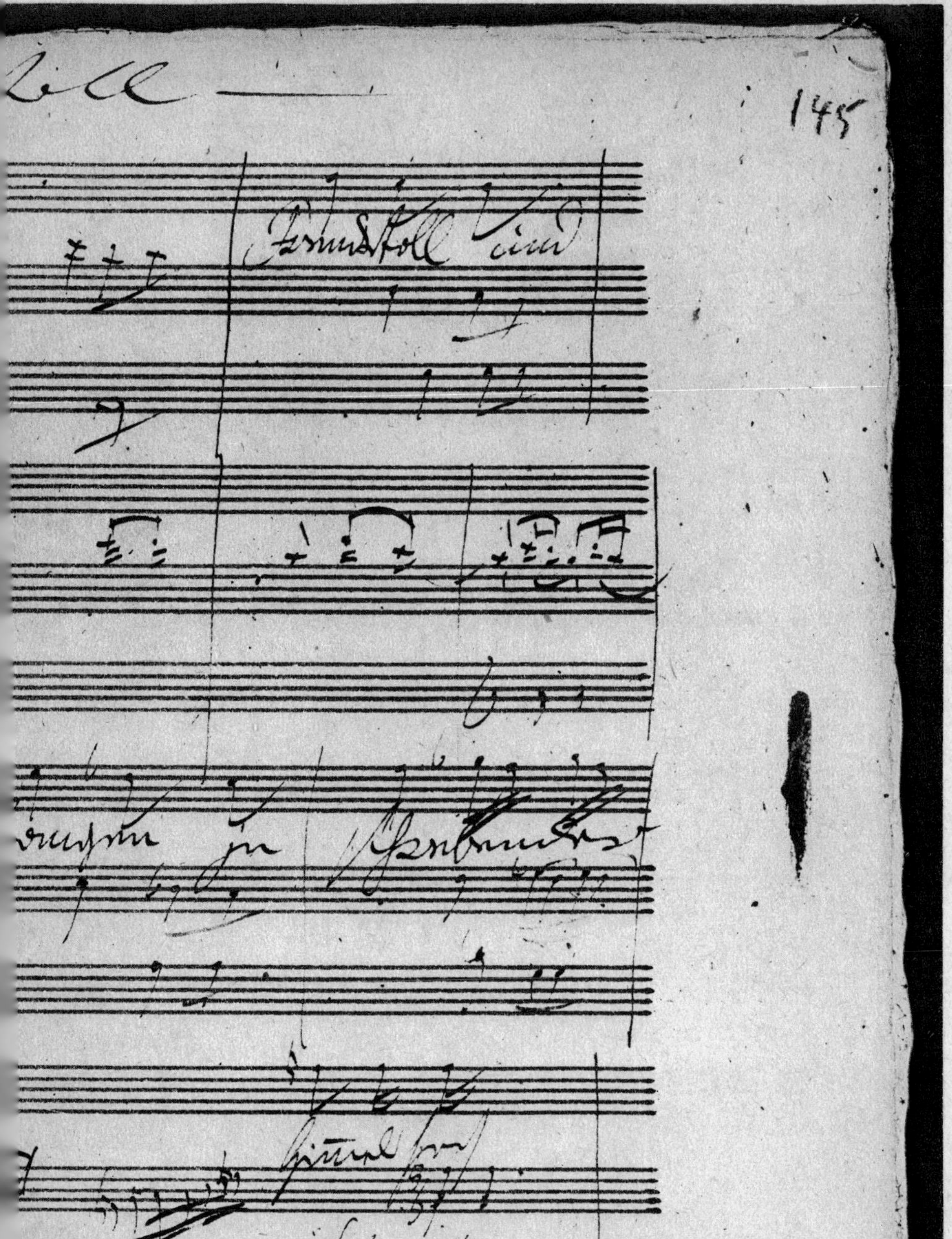
145

society man, very polite, stiff to the last degree, who always watched himself with a painful care lest he should unbend; who, after having heard Beethoven play (and we know what torrential floods his improvisations were), told him very courteously that he had played "most charmingly" (*"Er spielte köstlich"*).[62]

No doubt, Goethe, who was quite at a loss to express his appreciation of music, complimented the musician on his technique and on his clear-cut playing, with the air of one deeply impressed. But the æsthetic, the reasoned judgment which Beethoven looked for from a man like Goethe, was not forthcoming because Goethe had, in fact, none to offer; he did not understand. . . .

Beethoven exploded. . . .

Bettina describes the scene. She had not been there, but afterwards Beethoven ran hot foot, boiling with rage, to tell her of it. She, no doubt, succeeded in pouring oil on the fire.

Bettina had arrived in Teplitz on the evening of July 23rd with her husband and her sister, Mme. de Savigny. She did not know that she would find Goethe and Beethoven there. This meeting between the two, which she had so ardently desired, for which she had worked so tenaciously, had at last taken place. And, to her bitter disappointment, she was shut out. Goethe avoided her, all the more carefully because Christiana was watching him from afar.[63] No doubt Bettina had told the "Bacchus of music," as she nicknamed Beethoven, that she felt forsaken, like an Ariadne; and it is clear that Beethoven, very sensible of her charms and her faithful friendship, had taken her side.[64] There was no longer any reason to check the irritation which the evening with Goethe had roused in him; he expressed himself therefore without restraint.

Here is the extraordinary scene, written, or spoken, if you will, in the most genuine Beethoven style, in which the two great men appear to us in the most unexpected postures. For it was Goethe whose eyes filled with tears while Beethoven lectured him sharply on his sentimentality.

"He finished playing," wrote Bettina. "When he saw that Goethe was deeply moved, he said: 'Ah, sir, I had not expected that from you. . . . Long ago I gave a concert in Berlin. I had worked hard, and thought that I had done well. I expected a success, but when I had expended all my energy there was not the slightest sign of approval! . . . It was very painful, indeed, and I could not understand it. But I soon found the clue to the secret: The Berlin public was *fein gebildet* (fashionably cultured); in token of appreciation they waved their tear-sodden handkerchiefs at me. I saw that I had a "romantic,"[65] not an artistic, audience. . . .

But coming from you, Goethe, I do not like it. When your poems reach my brain I am filled with pride so intense that I long to climb to the height of your grandeur. No doubt, I was unable to rise to such a height . . . otherwise enthusiasm, in you, would have found a different mode of expression. Yet you yourself must know how stimulating it is to gain the applause of those possessed of understanding! If you do not recognize me, if you do not reckon me as your equal, who will? To what beggarly mob (*Bettelpack*) must I play to find understanding?' " . . .[66]

This was the first lesson he gave Goethe. What man had ever spoken to him before in such terms? . . . Bettina described Goethe's embarrassment, "for he knew perfectly well that Beethoven was right."[67]

From that moment, Beethoven was ill-disposed towards Goethe; even the smallest incident was not allowed to pass without comment.

They went out together, Beethoven taking Goethe's arm. In the streets of Teplitz and in the country lanes they often met aristocratic strollers. Goethe would bow ceremoniously, and this annoyed Beethoven; when he spoke of the court, of the empress, Goethe used "solemnly humble (*feierlich bescheiden*) expressions."[68]

"What are you up to?" (*"Ei was!"*) growled Beethoven. "You shouldn't do that. It is not right. You should throw boldly in their faces what you have in you, otherwise they will pay no attention. There is not a single princess who will recognize the genius of Tasso except from motives of vanity. That is not the way I treat them. When I was giving music lessons to the archduke, he once let me wait in the anteroom. So I rapped his knuckles, and when he asked why I was so impatient, I told him that I had wasted my time in his anteroom and had no patience left. After that he never kept me waiting. I would have made him feel the folly and stupidity of such bad manners (*Viehigkeit*). I told him: 'You may pin an order to anyone's breast; he will not be a fig the better for it. You can bestow the title of *Hofrat* or *Geheimrat*, but you will never make a Goethe, or a Beethoven, either. You must learn to appreciate, therefore, what you yourself are unable to create. It will be good for you (*Das ist Ihnen gesund*)'." . . .

That was the second lesson. We may imagine the frown with which Goethe, filled with respect for hierarchies and the social order, received it.

At this moment the empress, the dukes, and their suites came in sight, walking towards them. Beethoven said to Goethe:

"Let us walk on, arm in arm. They will have to get out of our way, not we out of theirs!"

Goethe did not approve of this, Bettina continues. The scene which she describes is well known. He broke away from Beethoven, and stood at the side of the road, hat in hand. Beethoven, swinging his arms, charged right through the midst of the princes, like a bull, merely touching his hat. They politely made room for him, and all greeted him in friendly fashion. When he had passed through them, Beethoven stopped and waited for Goethe, who was still bowing ceremoniously. Then he said to him:

"I have waited for you because I honour and esteem you, but you have honoured those people far too much."[69]

That was the third lesson, this time a practical one. It was a case of action as well as words. But now the measure was brimming over. The reproach may have been quite justified, but a man like Goethe could not allow his ears to be pulled like a schoolboy's!

Did Beethoven, we wonder, realize, even faintly, how many hard trials, bitter experiences, and dearly bought lessons were at the bottom of Goethe's social constraint and his tame acceptance of the order of things? Even if Beethoven were right, his manner of expressing his views would be intolerable!

Goethe wrote to Zelter (September 2, 1812):

"I have made Beethoven's acquaintance. His talent amazes me but, unfortunately, he has no self-control whatever. He is, no doubt, quite right in finding the world detestable, but by behaving as he does he really does not make it any more pleasant for himself or for others. We must forgive him a great deal, for his hearing is getting very bad; this interferes perhaps less with his musical than with his social side. He is naturally laconic, and he is becoming still more so as a result of his deafness."

Goethe's tone is very restrained. He could not have said less against Beethoven, and we must acknowledge his sense of justice.[70] Note his admission: "He is, no doubt, quite right in finding the world detestable."

Here again is Goethe's carefully repressed pessimism. Is there anyone who has deciphered Goethe's inner self? . . .

Who can have detected, under the poetic laurels heaped upon him, under the features of the gloomy Apollo which he wore, the bitter lines of his mouth, the marks of disappointment and disillusion, and the weaknesses so desperately concealed? This man detested emotion and abhorred the sight of disease and death;[71] the fissures in the social structure and in his own "ego," the possession by evil spirits—a constant obsession of his—caused him the utmost alarm; it was because he found them all within himself. Only his wisdom and self-control could erect the dikes which would save him from drowning.[72] Goethe, the monarch of life, knew only too well on what fragile foundations his empire rested, and what the building of it had cost him. Like the master builder in the old legend, he had walled into the heart of the structure many a woman's body! What a price did he pay, not for his egoistic peace of mind (as the vulgar call it, who cannot rise to such heights), but for the serenity of his work and its accomplishment. No doubt, he is not so robust, not so roughly hewn, not so virile as Beethoven. Beethoven's was one long fight; every step cost him dear; he was wounded again and again; he never wavered, but rushed, breast forward, straight upon the enemy. Goethe never fought, never argued. Pride and weakness both forbade a hand-to-hand encounter. He did not commit himself with the adversaries whom he despised nor, more dangerous still, with those whom he loved. He had but one resource, only one, always the same; when he met an obstacle, he fled, fled without even looking back. He effaced the recollection of the encounter from his sight and his mind.[73] His mental existence was a perpetual conquest, his life among men a constant flight. He stood aside and remained silent. . . .

But Beethoven would never realize this. Who did, in fact? Of all men, Beethoven would be the last to understand him.

After this meeting, Beethoven did not mince matters. He was certainly much less restrained than Goethe.

"Goethe is much too fond of the court atmosphere,[74] far fonder than is compatible with the dignity of a poet (*Goethe behagt die Hofluft zu sehr. Mehr als es einem Dichter ziemt*). If poets, who should be the foremost teachers (*Lehrer*) of a nation, can forget everything for dross such as this, let us never again refer to the foibles of musicians."[75]

He wrote this to his publishers. It was rash enough on his part to confide such impressions to strangers, but he did not leave it at that. Beethoven had one great weakness; when he had said something unpleasant to another, he was never content to let the matter rest there; he must publish it to the world at large.

After "giving Goethe a good talking-to" he hurried to the Arnims to tell them the "joke," for that was all it was—to him. "He was as pleased as a little boy at having 'teased' Goethe in this way."[76] We can guess whether the Arnims kept the "joke" to themselves! Their quarrel with Goethe had made them more intolerant of his weaknesses, and his abject attitude

C. F. ZELTER.
Direktor der Singakademie und Assessor der Königl.
Akademie der Künste in Berlin.
Den würdigen Mitgliedern der Singakademie gewidmet
von B. H. Bendix

towards the court displeased them; so they gave a lively account of it in their letters from Teplitz.[77]

It would not have mattered so much if Beethoven had restricted his gossip to Bettina's circle and to his own intimate friends. But he took the story with him wherever he went. The jeweller, Joseph Türck of Vienna, who during the season had a shop in Teplitz, told the following tale of Beethoven's joke with Goethe to all and sundry. While Goethe and Beethoven were walking out together, greeted at every step, Goethe said, rather pointedly, that he was tired of this constant bowing. Beethoven slyly remarked: "Don't be annoyed, Excellency. Perhaps they are bowing to me!"

We can imagine his hearty laugh, the laugh of a boy who has never grown up, his delight at having made a joke at His Excellency's expense. And, having had his laugh, he forgot the matter. . . .

He forgot it, but the joke went the rounds and returned to Goethe and Goethe did not laugh, nor did his devoted followers. . . .[78] The previous year Beethoven had formed a close friendship in Teplitz with the young Lieutenant Varnhagen von Ense and his "passion" Rahel, whose beautiful face recalled one who was dear to him.[79] On the German Olympus, where Bettina played the part of a daring little Hebe, sitting on his knees and drinking from Jupiter's cup like a honey bee, Rahel was Minerva, sprung from the god's head, standing on guard at the foot of the throne, ever watchful against possible familiarities. From the moment when Beethoven had dared to attack their god's prestige, Rahel and Varnhagen knew Beethoven no longer. Rahel never mentions him again in her diary.[80]

Silence. It is Goethe's deadly weapon, his mighty arm. He had given his Minerva lessons in this. He himself, too, was silent henceforth, and for many years never mentioned Beethoven. In 1813 Zelter, who had at last discovered the Overture to *Egmont*, spoke to Goethe of it.[81] Goethe made no reply.[82] Zelter, though eventually he found his "road to Damascus"[83] was not the man to exact from Goethe an admiration which was not in him.

One person only could hope to do this, by the right of her beauty and her love—Marianna von Willemer,[84] the Zuleika of the *Divan.* When her old lover sent her his *Lieder* from the *Divan*, set to music by some undistinguished composer, she had the courage to say, "Yes, no doubt it is quite nice, but . . .

". . . if I am to be quite frank, I should like Beethoven to write the melodies to these magnificent poems: he would understand them fully; nobody else could (*Sonst niemand*)! I felt that very strongly last winter, when I heard the music to *Egmont*; it is heavenly (*himmlisch*); he has absolutely grasped your meaning. It can almost be said that one and the same spirit has inspired (*beseelt*) your words and given life to (*belebt*) his music. . . ."[85]

Goethe replied[86] with his accustomed intelligence and amiability, that more often than not the music written to *Lieder* is misleading; the poet is rarely understood, and only the composer's mood (*Stimmung*) is conveyed.

"However," he adds, "I have also found many valuable works, in which I am clearly reflected (*vielmal abgespiegelt*); but the reflection is reduced or enlarged and is rarely quite true to life. In this respect Beethoven has accomplished miracles (*Beethoven hat darin Wunder gethan*)."

The praise is ambiguous. Goethe appears to see himself in Beethoven as if in a magnifying or distorting mirror.

Marianna, however, did not allow the matter to rest. A year later she returned to the charge. Speaking of the return of spring she wrote:

"If you would feel the new-born spring even more

intensely, ask some one with a beautiful soft voice to sing you Beethoven's *Lieder an die ferne Geliebte* (To the beloved distant). This music seems to me unsurpassable; the only other music to which it can be compared is that to *Egmont*. . . . But it must be sung simply and with feeling, and must be very well played. How I should like to know that it has given you pleasure and what you think of it."

We shall never know what he thought of it. But I like to think that the more conciliatory attitude and even the respect which Goethe showed for the name of Beethoven in 1820 and 1821 was due to this noble woman. It is true that he did not accept his art, but he no longer dismissed it with a word of contempt. He even made an effort, brief and not very serious, it is true, to understand him, and for this we must give him credit.

When young Johann Christian Lobe, who in spite of bashfulness had the courage of his convictions, dared to point out to him very respectfully how feeble and "*antiquiert*" (fossilized) Zelter's music was, and that the younger generation preferred the music of Beethoven and Weber, Goethe asked him to give his reasons, which Lobe did, very intelligently.[87]

"In Zelter's *Lieder*," he said, "the musical accompaniment is merely a harmonic and rhythmic filling-in.

18

Modern composers have given it the dignity of an auxiliary expression (*Mitsprache*) of the sentiment. If Goethe were to have only the bass and the accompaniment of one of Zelter's *Lieder* played to him, without the melody, he would find it difficult to discover the least connection between it and the sentiment. On the other hand, in the music of Beethoven and Weber the pulse-beats of the sentiment (*Leben und Regung des Gefühls*) can be clearly felt in the accompaniment. And yet this is only the babbling (*Lallen*) of music's childhood. Music will one day reach a stage in which each note of the accompaniment will play an integral part in the expression of the sentiment."

Here we find a prophecy of the task of Wagner's orchestra, a prophecy made in 1820!

Goethe listened, silent and attentive, with bowed head. Then he went to the piano, opened it, and said: "Give me an example. If your deductions are correct, you should be able to prove them."

Lobe then played the accompaniment of a *Lied* by Zelter, and that of the *Lied* from *Egmont*, Drums and Fifes (*Trommeln und Pfeifen*). After that he played the two melodies.

No doubt Goethe was not convinced and was only too ready to condemn the new tendencies on the strength of this isolated example, which may perhaps have been played indifferently.[88] Still, it was a great deal for him to go even so far as to seek information. If practice did not interest him, theory did.

Some months later, at the end of September, 1820, Goethe received F. Foerster, a musician from Berlin. Talking to him of the wrong interpretation which Prince Radziwill had given to a dialogue from *Faust* which the latter had set to music, Goethe pointed out the perfect appropriateness of Beethoven's music to Egmont's monologue in the prison scene.[89] He recited the monologue in a moving fashion and said:

"Here I have added a note that the music is to play while the hero falls asleep. Beethoven understood me and interpreted most admirably my meaning (*Beethoven ist mit bewunderungswerten Genie in meine Intentionen eingegangen*)."

A year later the poet Ludwig Rellstab, who was one of Beethoven's great admirers,[90] had a conversation with Goethe (the end of October, 1821):

"We spoke a great deal of Beethoven, whom he knew personally. He was proud to possess some of his manuscripts. On this occasion he sent for Geheimrat Schmidt to play a sonata by Beethoven."[91]

We see, then, that Beethoven's music was by no means banned from his house as often has been stated. Here is a further proof.

At the beginning of November, 1821, a few days after Rellstab's first visit, Goethe invited a gathering of friends to listen to young Mendelssohn, then a boy of twelve. Rellstab gives us a vivid account of this event. After the child artist had played and improvised admirably, Goethe fetched some of his precious autograph manuscripts.

"Now, look at this, my boy! This will beat you." And he placed on the piano the manuscript of a *Lied* by Beethoven.[92] The writing was almost illegible! Mendelssohn burst into laughter.

Said Goethe, "Guess who wrote that."

And Zelter, unpleasant as usual, replied: "Beethoven. He always writes as if he used a broomstick for a pen."

On hearing this, young Felix was struck silent with awe. It was a sudden seriousness; it was more; it was "a solemn marvelling" (*heiliges Staunen*); his eyes were fixed, riveted. . . . Gradually an expression of "joyous wonder illumined his face, as little by little he unravelled from the crabbed writing the lofty melody, like the sun rising in splendour." Goethe's eyes, radiant with joy (*freudestrahlend*) never left his face. So impatient was he that he did not give him time to collect his thoughts:

"You see, you see, if I hadn't told you, you would have been caught. . . . Come now, try it."

Felix began to play hesitatingly; he stopped, corrected his mistakes, discussing them aloud, played to the end, then played the piece again, this time right through without interruption. During the whole evening Goethe was overjoyed, and never ceased to discuss the feat with his guests.

This shows how exaggerated has been the supposed ostracism of Beethoven's music in the house at Weimar. Goethe thought so little of his estrangement with Beethoven that when, in 1822, the young French violinist Alexandre Boucher, fearing that Beethoven would not consent to receive him in spite of his letters of introduction, sought Goethe's assistance in the matter, the latter gave him a note to Beethoven, which at once opened to him the doors of the great composer's house (April 29, 1822).[93]

How then are we to explain Goethe's extraordinary silence when Beethoven, in 1823, unwell and worried by lack of money, wrote him a letter in the humblest terms (February 8th) asking him to speak on his behalf to the Grand Duke of Weimar, and beg him to subscribe for the publication of his *Missa Solemnis?* On reading this entreaty we feel a sense of shame, not so much for the writer, as for the recipient; it is painful to see a great man humiliate himself.

What a moving effort this was, to interest Goethe in

his humble domestic life, and in his sixteen-year-old nephew, whose knowledge of Greek he proudly praised ("But it is very expensive to educate a boy"). What respectful affection he expressed for Goethe, what vivid recollections of "the happy hours spent in his company," what "Adoration, love, and high esteem" (*"Verehrung, Liebe, und Hochachtung"*), which the awkward wording makes even more touching, and, above all, what fear that the expression of this affection and the dedication to Goethe of the two great works *Meeresstille*, and *Glückliche Fahrt*,[94] might give the impression of having been prompted by mercenary reasons. It seems as if no generously-minded man could even for a single day have left the sting of suffering to rankle in a noble and confiding heart. One would have thought that even if Goethe had no interest whatever in a *Missa Solemnis*, he would have opened his arms to Beethoven, saying:

"I thank you for having come to me for help. Make no apologies. If you humble yourself before me, it is I whom am humbled."

Goethe never replied. For this his enemies find a very convenient explanation. They say that he was "unkind";[95] his admirers in their embarrassment avoid the question, and state that his health was very poor.

And, indeed, about the month of February, 1823,

Goethe became seriously ill; but let us enquire into the circumstances more closely.

Beethoven's letter arrived in Weimar on February 15th. Goethe had been feeling unwell since the 13th. By the 18th he was very ill, even dangerously so. As was always the case with Goethe, any illness came on very suddenly and violently, but usually did not last long. For eight days and eight nights he never left his armchair; he was feverish and delirious. His two medical advisers were very concerned, and he himself told them: "You will not be able to save me. Death is waiting for me; death is lurking at every corner. I am lost." Nevertheless, he struggled on. He showed on the tenth day that he was recovering by inveighing furiously against his doctors, who had forbidden him a certain beverage which he wanted. "If I am to die, I want to die in my own way." He had his drink and felt better. Before the end of the month he was already speaking of his illness as if it were a matter of ancient history, and he soon took up his old life—and how vehemently!

Goethe was then seventy-five. He fell in love with a girl of nineteen, Ulrike von Levetzow. He spent the months of June and July with her, at Marienbad; this love affair upset him as if he had been a young man; for no reason whatever, he would weep; music reduced him to tears. One month of separation was more than

19

20

he could endure. In September he met the Levetzows again in Karlsbad, and the old man danced with the girls. Do not let us accuse him of senility. The passionate, the great, the magnificent *Elegie* which his torments inspired is a glorious work; it possesses the overwhelming passion, displayed in *Werther*, and the plenitude of art which distinguishes the great works of his maturity. He lived in a tempest, and scattered the tempest about him. There were some very unpleasant scenes at home; his son became furious when he heard that the old man intended to marry again. When he asked for the hand of Ulrike her parents politely dissuaded him. Goethe was deeply distressed. Towards the end of the year he was again stricken by serious illness. In his house nobody looked after him. Zelter, who came unexpectedly to see him, was horrified when he saw how abandoned was his old friend. The two old men fell into each other's arms and opened their hearts to each other. Goethe confessed how unhappy he was. His last dream of joy was broken; henceforth he would have to live a life of renunciation in deadly loneliness. "If Goethe had died then," writes Emil Ludwig, "he would have died a vanquished man."

Goethe lived, thank God, and soon he cut, as it were,

in the glacier of his grief steps by which he rose to summits which hitherto he had never attained.

We see, however, that if his illness in February was an inadequate reason for disregarding Beethoven's letter, the upsetting events of the year, and the fevered weakness of his disordered heart, explain how, in the midst of all this storm and turmoil, Beethoven's request was overlooked. It may, of course, be contended that this passionate egoism lacked the resources of love and charity which would have provided him with a noble diversion from his own sufferings, in alleviating those of others. But when we realize that this boundless egoism, the mirror of the universe, was the guiding principle of a world-wide intelligence, of a spirit full of light and beauty, we no longer dare to condemn it. As well condemn the lordly indifference of the sun.

My blame is reserved for Zelter, the faithful but timid friend. For mediocrity cannot claim the excuses which we make for genius. If mediocrity be not good and loyal, what else can be said for it? Zelter was all the more in duty bound to remind Goethe of Beethoven's request because he himself knew of Beethoven's letter and understood its pathetic appeal. Since he had met Beethoven in 1819 his feelings towards him had undergone a complete change. An excellent man, though unprepossessing, Zelter had been moved to tears by Beethoven's physical disabilities and by his kindness.[96] From that time he showed him a brotherly devotion; he subscribed to the *Missa Solemnis*, and put his *Singchor* of 160 voices, which was then the best choral society in Germany, at Beethoven's disposal; henceforth he included regularly in his programs the works of the great composer whom he now compared to Michelangelo.

And yet, so weak and cowardly is man, he was careful not to mention the *Missa Solemnis* to Goethe. And, when Beethoven died, Zelter did not dare to speak of him to Goethe, although in secret his soul saluted the shade of the demigod. It would appear that during the whole year the name of Beethoven was never mentioned between them.[97]

How terrible, how inhuman is this silence, yet who can tell how often Goethe himself had laid the tombstone of silence upon death, burying thus his secret thoughts with the death of his nearest and dearest. At the age of sixty he said to Riemer:[98]

"Only those with the acutest sensibility can prove excessively hard and excessively cold. They must, as it were, don thick armour in order to ward off harsh assaults, and only too often does this armour weigh heavily upon them."

To hide is, with Goethe, an instinctive method of

defence; the imperious call to concealment sometimes disguises his anxiety. At the same time his genial superiority turns this instinct into the impulse which gave rise to his most moving lyric flights. The whole nature of the man was an instrument which he sacrificed in the service of art and thought. He thrust aside his sorrows, his loves, and his fears. . . . Who, indeed, harboured more sorrow, love, and fear than this Faust, so intrepid and restless, round whom the Satanic poodle* ran in magic circles. . . . The symbolic poodle who, in old age, never left the shadow of his steps?

I have in my possession a beautiful letter from Goethe to Wilhelm von Humboldt, written on October 22, 1826, a few months before Beethoven's death. Humboldt was trying to dissuade Goethe from his attitude of aloofness on the subject of Indian philosophy. Goethe answered:

"I have nothing whatever against Indian thought, but I am afraid of it (*aber ich fürchte mich davor*). It would involve my imagination in the pursuit of the formless and the misshapen (*denn es zieht meine Einbildungskraft ins Formlose und Difforme*); I must guard myself more earnestly than ever against this (*wovor ich mich mehr als jemals zu hüten habe*)."[99]

* TRANSLATOR'S NOTE.—Romain Rolland refers here to Mephistopheles in Goethe's great poem, who first approaches Faust in the form of a poodle, running in circles round his victim and drawing closer and closer.

Always and ever more keenly, as his life draws to its end, does he feel this secret attraction and the fear of the abyss.

For Goethe, Beethoven was the abyss.

The famous scene of which Mendelssohn has told us proves this. It shows us the old man's apprehension, and his desperate fight to keep behind bars the savage demons which, many years later, were to bring the aged Tolstoi low when he wrote the *Kreutzer Sonata.*

It was in 1830, three years after Beethoven's death. "In the morning I had to play to him, for nearly an hour, music by the great composers in chronological order. . . . He was sitting in a dark corner like a Jupiter with his thunderbolts. From time to time lightning flashes darted from his old eyes. He refused to let me mention Beethoven, but I told him that I could not help it, and played the first movement of the C Minor Symphony. This moved him strangely. At first he said: 'This does not cause any emotion, only astonishment (*das bewegt aber gar nichts, das macht nur staunen*); it is superb!' For a while he continued to growl in this way. Then, after a long silence, he went on: 'It is stupendous, absolutely mad. It makes me almost fear that the house will collapse. And supposing the whole of mankind played it at once! . . .[100] (*Das ist sehr gross, ganz toll! Man möchte sich fürchten das*

Haus fiele ein. Und wenn das nun alle die Menschen zusammen spielen!)' . . . Later on, during dinner, he started growling again. . . ."

The stroke had gone home. He should have admitted it, but he refused to do so. He was compelled to cheat, so that the ordered destiny of his thought might be fulfilled.

The conclusion to which I have come, is this: Of the two men, the exalted and often wavering Beethoven-Dionysus and Goethe, the Olympian, it is Goethe who concealed the greater moral weakness. But only those possessing the strongest character recognize their own weakness and fix the boundaries of their spiritual dominion. Beethoven's dominion was the boundless sky (*Mein Reich ist in der Luft*). Hence his extraordinary fascination and his generosity, hence also the dangers about him. The century of music which came after him fell a victim to them. Only Wagner was strong enough to take up and grasp the sceptre which the sorcerer apprentices* had allowed to fall to the ground.[101]

* TRANSLATOR'S NOTE.—Romain Rolland refers here to *Der Zauberlehrling* ("The sorcerer-apprentice"), a magnificent poem by Goethe. The theme is that an apprentice—*i.e.*, one who is not a master of his profession, should refrain from attempting to do great things, otherwise disaster will follow.

Beethoven, however, was never aware of the dangers which he let loose. Nor did he guess, let us hope, the existence of the secret dislike which separated him from the great man whom he venerated more than any other mortal. That he should have suffered from Goethe's obstinate silence and his failure to reply to his letters we can well understand. Yet Beethoven, so easily roused to anger, who would not tolerate from anyone, even were he one of the world's masters, the neglect of the consideration to which he was entitled, never showed any sign of resentment at Goethe's incomprehensible attitude. Never once did he complain. In his *Conversation Note-Book** of 1819 we read that once somebody in his presence attempted to speak disparagingly of Goethe: "Goethe should give up writing; the fate which awaits singers who have grown old will overtake him, too."

No doubt Beethoven must have interrupted him violently with words of protest, for the other person apologized and hastened to write, "He remains, nevertheless, Germany's greatest poet."[102]

The days at Teplitz are not forgotten; but all that Beethoven remembers of them is the light; the shadows of the scene have all disappeared. The memory of

* TRANSLATOR'S NOTE.—Beethoven was then completely deaf. His visitors wrote whatever they wished to say into his note-book. He would then answer aloud.

Goethe's weaknesses is gone; his own scoffing and teasing he has frankly forgotten. Of Goethe he remembers only his greatness and his kindness.

"So you know the great Goethe?" he exclaimed in a conversation with Rochlitz (1822). He beat his breast, beaming with joy, "I know him, too; I met him in Karlsbad[103] God knows how long ago. I was not as deaf as I am today, but my hearing was even then very poor. How patient the great man was with me. You can hardly believe how happy it made me. I would have given my life for him ten times over."

Thus each passed on his way without clear view of the other. Beethoven, whose love was the greater, could but wound his friend. Goethe, whose insight was the keener, never understood the one who was nearest to him, the great man who alone was his peer, who alone was worthy of his friendship and his love.

"We all make mistakes, but everyone makes different mistakes," wrote the dying Beethoven on his bed of suffering, like old King Lear.[104]

GOETHE'S SILENCE

GOETHE (1810)

DRAWING BY FRIEDRICH WILHELM RIEMER

21

GOETHE'S SILENCE

"Silence! It is Goethe's deadly weapon, his mighty arm." I wrote these words in 1927 in my essay on Goethe's attitude towards Beethoven, after their meeting in Teplitz—that is from the end of 1812 to Beethoven's death.

Since then I have made a closer study of the subject, with a more intimate knowledge of Goethe's musical life during these fifteen years (1812-27). I have ventured further into the dark secrets of his silence. Here is the result of my latest researches.

The outstanding discovery is this:

During this period of fifteen years Goethe, at Weimar, had all the means of obtaining abundant information about Beethoven, about both the man and his work. There is every good reason to believe that he did obtain it.

From 1813 Goethe's constant companion was a close friend of his, Johann Heinrich Friedrich Schütz, an inspector of Berka Spa, a three hours' journey from Weimar. Schütz was an excellent pianist and organist. They often met and Schütz played to him the works of German composers, hour after hour. It is true that he preferred Bach to any other, and that he inspired Goethe with the same devotion. But he also played Beethoven frequently.

There was another intimate friend of Goethe's, who was entirely and singly devoted to Beethoven—the Secret Councillor of State (*Geheimer Regierungsrat*) Friedrich Schmidt. This amiable and worthy man was an enthusiastic apostle. He wrote sonnets, dedicated to Beethoven's works. He knew his sonatas by heart, and played Beethoven almost exclusively, probably, as Ferdinand Hiller tells us in his memoirs, "with more intelligence than technique." "This was perhaps not the best means of propaganda for the master," he writes: nevertheless, it is worth noticing that Goethe never showed any objection to listen to him.

In 1817 there arrived in Weimar a musician of considerable reputation, who installed himself there permanently as *Kapellmeister*, Johann Nepomuk Hummel. He was the most famous piano virtuoso of his time. Hummel, who was then forty years old, had had the privilege of being Mozart's only pupil, and he was both a rival and friend of Beethoven's. They had met when very young, in 1787 as a matter of fact, when Hummel was nine years old, and Beethoven seventeen. As virtuosi in Vienna, about the year 1802, they often joined in friendly rivalry; and Karl Czerny has handed down to us an account of these contests which divided society into opposite camps. Both were remarkable in improvisation, but their manner of playing differed greatly. Hummel was a master of good taste and elegance, and his execution was clear cut and clean: probably no one ever equalled him in the interpretation of Mozart's music. Beethoven, on the other hand, excelled in the play of his imagination, the energy of his rhythm, his ardour, and his control of the mighty impulses which he released. It is to the credit of the two virtuosi that their rivalry did not affect their friendship. It is true that occasionally some small misunderstanding occurred, when Beethoven would send Hummel one of those terrible letters of his, in which he poured a stream of invective on the head of his astonished friend, only to beg him, in the warmest terms, on the same evening or the next morning, to come and be friends again.[105] The good-humoured Hummel never allowed these incidents to interfere with their friendship. From 1804 to 1811 he deputized for and later became the successor of, Haydn, in the household of Prince Esterhazy at Eisenstadt. And when in 1807 Beethoven came there for the performance of his Mass in C, and the prince exclaimed, "My dear Beethoven, what on earth have you concocted now?" Hummel could not hide a smile, thereby drawing upon himself the thunderbolts of wrath which Beethoven could not launch against the princely head. Schindler, a very worthy man, but possessing no sense of humour, concluded, quite mistakenly, that this incident led to a lasting estrangement. So far was this from being the case that in 1813-14 we find Hummel gallantly conducting the drums and cannon of his warlike friend's army in the *Schlachtensymphonie* (*the Battle of Vittoria*), while Beethoven wrote him facetious Napoleonic proclamations. Hummel continued to be the faithful friend, who immediately, on hearing of Beethoven's last illness, hurried from Weimar to Vienna, and remained at the bedside of the dying man. We shall find him there presently. . . . We see, then, that Beethoven could not have had a more illustrious advocate at Weimar than Hummel. We are told that the virtuosi of that time were not in the habit of playing any other compositions than their own; there were,

22

however, exceptions, and there is no doubt that Hummel proved, for society in Weimar, a veritable mine of Beethoven lore. It is therefore difficult to believe that he never spoke of Beethoven to Goethe, who met him frequently and was curiously influenced by Hummel's powers of musical fascination.[106] Goethe, in his wisdom, always attached great importance to the judgment of the professional musician, and was thus bound to take note of the great appreciation which Hummel professed for Beethoven, even if he himself did not share it.

Then Zelter, Goethe's Achates, went to Vienna during the summer of 1819: he met Beethoven on the way. In spite of his rugged exterior he was a kindly-hearted man, and Beethoven's physical sufferings affected him very deeply; the old friends fell into each other's arms. ". . . (*Und ich habe kaum die Tränen verhalten können*—I could hardly restrain my tears)."[107]

From this moment Zelter always showed kindness to the unfortunate man of genius, who displayed the deepest gratitude to him, a gratitude which was perhaps out of proportion to the actual value of the services rendered.

Through Goethe's house there passed a continuous stream of distinguished visitors—musicians, men of taste, well-known critics, men personally acquainted with Beethoven—who have left us interesting accounts of their conversation with him: Wenzel Tomaschek, who had set some of Goethe's poems to music; Rellstab, later the sponsor of the *Moonlight Sonata*; above all, Johann Friedrich Rochlitz, the foremost musical historian of the time and for thirty years Goethe's friend and correspondent, who has spoken so nobly of Beethoven, and to whom Beethoven confided, in 1822, his unbounded affection for Goethe.[108]

But there is more to tell, and I must resume the story of the year 1823, that year of tragedy, when Beethoven, harassed by ill-fortune, knocked vainly at Goethe's door; I have already quoted his humble appeal, which Goethe, a prey to both the desire of love and the fear of death, seemed to disregard. When I first pictured this scene, I did not sufficiently emphasize the pathetic character of these months of infinite sadness (*Wehmut*) when "all seemed lost" for Goethe, and when "he himself was lost."[109] Goethe's heart was never more accessible to music and to musical emotion than in this very year when he left Beethoven at his door; it was as if fate had ironically determined to render ridiculous the misunderstanding which made Goethe turn a deaf ear to his friend.

His senile love for the nineteen-year-old little Ulrike was only one indication of the restlessness which was then consuming Goethe. In Marienbad this restlessness came under music's influence. At no other period of his life did the sound of music overwhelm him to such a degree; he himself was at a loss to understand it. Two great women artists thrilled the old man's heart far more than the colourless Ulrike. They were Anna Milder-Hauptmann—Beethoven's Leonora—whose singing of the simplest song moved Goethe to tears;[110] and even more, an enchanting Polish pianist, Marie Szymanowska, then thirty-three years of age. He dreamed for many months of this "ravishing, all-powerful mistress of tone" (*"die zierliche Ton-Allmächtige"*).

But it needed not the art of Muses as fair as these to overcome him. Even an open-air concert given by the band of the local infantry regiment was enough to upset him.[111] This worried him, and he tried to find an explanation of his emotion; it almost seemed as if he were ashamed and afraid of it.

His letter to Zelter, in which he told his old friend of his state of mind, sounds almost apologetic. . . . He maintained that for the last two years he had not heard any music—in this he was either wrong or trying to deceive himself. Suddenly music assailed him and released the winged messengers of recollections long forgotten. It was too much. . . . "I am convinced that, if I were to go to a concert by your *Singakademie* I should have to leave the hall after the first bar. Ah, when I think," he continued, "of the happiness which I should derive from hearing every week an opera like *Don Juan!* I know now what sorrow it is to be deprived of a delight which lifts man out of himself, out of the world, to greater heights. How I need it, how splendid it would be if I were with you. You would heal my morbid sensitiveness (*krankhaften Reizbarkeit*), and little by little enable me to assimilate once more God's greatest revelation (*die ganze Fülle der schönsten Offenbarung Gottes in mich aufzunehmen*). Instead of this, I shall have to spend a winter empty of music and form (*klang und formlosen Winter*) and I am afraid of it (*vor dem mir doch gewissermassen graut*). . . ."

This great man, now so old and immured in the cold walls of solitude, who can fail to be deeply moved at hearing his confession? . . . But what is it that isolates him? And what strange fear is it that makes him dread the thought of leaving his prison? Germany was full of friends eager to see him. In Berlin his faithful friend Zelter was anxiously awaiting his coming; he had been waiting for twenty years past; and the whole of Berlin, the Court, the élite, and the crowds among whom Zelter's and Reichardt's *Lieder* had spread his fame and given rise to a loving veneration of his name,

Göethe.

all were eagerly expecting him. But he never came; he was never to see Vienna. He is on the defensive . . . but against what? Is it happiness? Is it glory? Or is it the gaping crowd which he shuns? . . . How little self-assurance he has! But he knows what manner of man he is and we know what a masterpiece he carved out of his very being. He is wise and recognizes the abysses which he must avoid.

So he returned to his winter quarters in Thuringia, frozen to the very heart. He complained that all that was left for him was to bury himself in his retreat and await shivering the return of summer, which would allow him to resume in Bohemia the only life worth living. . . .

And just then suddenly there appeared on October 24th the queen of the snows, the enchantress Szymanowska.[112]

There followed twelve days of pure delight, twelve days devoted to the most sacred emotions of beauty, of tenderness, and of music. The accents of almost religious gratitude in which Goethe praised her to the skies, the charming words with which he bade his visitor farewell on the eve of her departure, are evidence of the profound joy which her presence and her inspired playing had given him. . . .[113]

It has, however, not been sufficiently recognized that

in these sacred feasts of art Beethoven occupied an important place. On October 27th a Beethoven trio was played at Goethe's house. On November 4th, in the great concert given at the Stadthaus in honour of Szymanowska, Beethoven figures twice on the program. The concert opened with the Fourth Symphony in B Flat, and after the interval his quintet, op. 16 for piano, oboe, clarinet, horn, and bassoon, was played. Thus Beethoven had the lion's share, and without mentioning his name, Goethe confessed to Knebel that he was again "completely carried away by the whirlwind of sounds (*da bin ich nun wieder in den Strudel der Töne hineingerissen*)." Thus there had been opened to him a new world, the world of modern music which he had hitherto refused to accept—"*durch Vermittelung eines Wesens, das Genüsse, die man immer ahndet und immer entbehrt, zu verwirklichen geschaffen ist* (through the medium of one who has the gift of endowing with life those delights which we resent and of which we deprive ourselves)."

The following incident shows how deep was the emotion in the old man's heart at this time. On the evening of November 5th Mme. Szymanowska came to bid him good-bye. Goethe kissed her without a word; his eyes dwelt upon her as she walked away. He turned to Councillor van Müller and said: "I have much to thank her for . . . she has given me back to myself (*mich zuerst mir selbst wiedergegeben*)."

He went to bed at an early hour, feeling worn out. The next morning he had a heart attack. He had violent fits of coughing; he felt as if he were going to die. When Zelter arrived on November 24th it seemed to him a house of death that he entered; he was paralyzed with fear. For twenty days he remained closeted with his old friend who confided all his troubles to him. They spoke also of music. Zelter mentioned that Haydn was writing some "joyous" masses, and that when some one had expressed surprise at this new style of sacred music he had replied: "When I think of God I always feel so indescribably happy. . . ." And tears, healing tears, again flowed over Goethe's cheeks.

On December 13th Zelter left, and again Goethe took up his life and its tasks.

Thus we see how filled with tenderness, emotion, and melancholy was the Goethe of that time, how deeply music affected him. I was wrong, therefore, in saying, as I did, that during these tempestuous months the thought of Beethoven had altogether vanished. No, the spirit of Beethoven, too, had been heard amid the storm. . . .

All the more extraordinary is it, therefore, that Goethe, after his recovery, never spoke of him.

Just then death knocked at Beethoven's door.

At the first news of the danger, Hummel, the Weimar *Hofkapellmeister* and a cherished friend of Goethe, left to bid a last farewell to his great fellow artist, taking with him his wife and his young pupil, Ferdinand Hiller, for whom Goethe showed a fatherly affection. They arrived in time to find Beethoven still fully conscious and happy to see the old couple again. They embraced each other and they talked. Hummel and Hiller paid four visits (February 28, March 13, March 20, March 23, 1827).[114] Each time they found him weaker. The sun was setting. At the last visit the sufferer could no longer speak; his teeth were clenched in the supreme struggle. Frau Hummel bent over him and wiped the sweat from the dying man's brow. Beethoven's expression at this moment had a striking effect on young Hiller. Forty years later he wrote: "I shall never forget the look of gratitude in those broken eyes (*sein gebrochenes Auge*) as he turned them on her."

Three days later Beethoven died. Hummel was present at the funeral. On April 9th he returned to Weimar,[115] and met Goethe again. . . .

24

Nothing. . . . Goethe asked no questions. . . . Goethe found nothing to say. . . .[116]

Nothing? Yes, he did say something—a year later. And it was all he ever said on this subject.

In 1828, in his report on the *Monatschrift der Gesellschaft des vaterländischen Museums in Böhmen*, Goethe wrote, in stilted fashion:

"Mention should be made of the 'Requiem' by Tomaschek, to which we shall refer separately in greater detail, because it is one of the most recent creations of the famous composer; we should also make honourable mention of the religious service held in Prague on the occasion of Beethoven's death" (*"So wie zugleich der für Beethoven veranstalteten kirchlichen Totenfeier ehrend Erwähnung zu tun"*).

His pen had compelled him to write the name "Beethoven" . . . *"ehrend Erwähnung! . . ."*

And this is the *single reference* to Beethoven in the whole of Goethe's writings!

"Nil mirari."

Whatever we may feel, let us do as Goethe did—let us try and understand.

In all that we have noted not a trace of personal hostility is to be found. The thought of Beethoven, whose mind and person had for a moment fascinated him, no doubt distressed and troubled him; so Goethe put it from his mind. It would, however, be utterly false to maintain that he ever showed the slightest dislike for him.

There are other great musicians whom physically Goethe could not tolerate. Weber, for instance, whose last visit (July, 1825), just before his death, leaves us a terrible impression. Weber, already suffering from his last illness, was announced. He was kept waiting in the antechamber. Twice afterwards he was asked for his name, a name famous throughout Germany since the triumph of his opera *Freischütz* in Berlin in 1821, and even in Weimar in 1822. Goethe had heard it in 1824, as well as *Euryanthe.* When at last he was admitted to Goethe's presence he found "a man of stone," ice-cold and stern, who spoke to him with a frigid politeness on matters of no moment. Not a word was said of his music. Weber left, deeply hurt, went to bed shaking with fever, remained in bed at his hotel for two days without anyone troubling about him, and left Weimar forever.

This was a case of Goethe's dislike for the whole man with all his attributes. He disliked Weber's person, his leanness, his sickliness, his grotesque shape, his perpetual snuffling, his ugly spectacles; the whole wretched appearance of the man irritated the Olympian: he disliked his mind, the mind of the self-appointed mouthpiece of the national and military instincts of the vulgar, which Goethe despised. He disliked his noisy, rowdy music—"A lot of noise for nothing," Goethe grumbled as he left the theatre after the second act of *Oberon.* Finally he disliked the man who set stupid poems to music; this was an unforgivable offence in Goethe's eyes, and we may add that on this last point Beethoven condemned Weber with equal severity.

There is nothing of this kind in the case of Beethoven. Let us remember Goethe's feeling of respect and astonishment when he first met Beethoven (1812):

"Zusammengefasster, energischer, inniger habe ich noch keinen Künstler gesehen."

Beethoven made a great impression on Goethe. But the latter feared him; it was apprehension of a claim to equality, a claim which he must set aside.

Goethe was too noble to refuse to admit equality in others. For him it should have been rather a reason for seeking out Beethoven.

Was it his music, then, that he disliked?

In all our researches we have not found a single fact suggesting that Beethoven's music was not frequently performed in Weimar, either at concerts or at the theatre, or, for that matter, even at Goethe's own house. Under the very direction of Goethe performances of

Egmont were given at the Weimar Theatre, with Beethoven's incidental music.[117] And in 1816 he produced *Fidelio*.[118] Whether he liked this music or not, he respected the composer's artistic rights and independence; he would never have hindered his triumphal progress.

Besides, Beethoven's greatness was already established. After 1815 it was an accomplished fact. The examples which I quoted in my first essay prove that in 1820 and 1821 Goethe himself expressed his esteem. Beethoven, as represented by *Egmont*, is certainly beyond discussion.

I may add that on no occasion did Goethe ever refuse, from mere prejudice, to listen to those who desired and were qualified to teach him something. His highly developed scientific mind imposed this upon him. He was not one of those poets who in idle pride despise the lessons of history.[119] As I shall show later, no other writer showed a greater and more sustained interest in art and particularly in the history of music. The comprehension of a work of art seemed to him impossible without a perception of its proper place in the chain of evolution of form and mind.[120] And in that chain of evolution Goethe's personal predilection did not react against this or that particular work. His intelligence alone was concerned; it observed the facts, deduced with lucidity the laws governing them, and accepted these laws with serenity. He never missed an opportunity of organizing in Weimar musical performances in historic cycles with commentaries and thus presented the finest examples of music of the different epochs. In 1818 Schütz, of Berka, played for him during three consecutive weeks, for three or four hours every day, German compositions for the piano from Handel and Bach to Beethoven. In 1830 Mendelssohn, at his request, played for him for a fortnight all the classical composers from the beginning of the eighteenth century to the *"grossen neuen Technikern"* ("the great modern technicians") of whom, as Goethe wrote to Zelter, he gave him "a sufficient idea" (*"hinreichende Begriffe"*). And there is no doubt that among these "great modern technicians" Beethoven had the place of honour.[121]

I feel convinced that Goethe did not deny him this place. I have said elsewhere that in all technical questions concerning an art other than his own, Goethe was loyal enough to accept the judgment of those whom he recognized as more competent than himself. Now, about the year 1825 I fail to find any musician of importance in Goethe's circle—Rochlitz, Schütz, Mendelssohn, Lobe, Tomaschek, Rellstab, even Zelter—who did not recognize Beethoven's musical genius, whatever may have been the criticisms which one or another expressed of his work.

What, then, is the conclusion?

It is this, that Goethe admitted, recognized, even admired his greatness, but did not like it.

That is the whole point. Can we blame him? No man can love to order. Goethe in his affection and his art was always sincere.

His predilection in music we shall see later. It is a fine, one might even say an enormous, field. It extends from the popular *Lied* to the choral polyphony of the Italian sixteenth century, from Palestrina to Bach, from *Don Juan* to the *Barber*; the heroic oratorios of Handel were enthroned in the very centre of his affections side by side with the "Well-tempered Clavichord"; I know few poets of whom as much could be said.

But there were two things which he did not like, two types of music, the colossal and the melancholy romantic. To be crushed or to be depressed was to him equally unendurable.

A third matter, entirely physiological, influenced his judgment; his ear could not tolerate "too much noise." This was one of the reasons why he did not leave home during his last years, going to the theatre only on very rare occasions. The new music induced in him physical suffering. He would listen to orchestral music only if it was arranged for the piano.

This suggests the true meaning of the exclamation which I quoted earlier in this book, after Mendelssohn had played the first movement of the C Minor Symphony.

"Und wenn das nun alle die Menschen zusammen spielen" (Supposing the whole of mankind played it at once).

We can picture him making off, his hands clapped over his ears.

Is it astonishing? In 1830 Goethe was the man who long, long ago as a boy, had heard the seven-year-old Mozart play. He was descended from the far-off golden age, and the development of his organic sensibility could not keep pace with the growth of his intelligence.

Now when a man's senses can no longer appreciate works of art without pain and suffering, his intelligence inclines him to the belief that here is an art which must inevitably crush and depress him. Goethe therefore put it from him. In so doing he put Beethoven from him.

To every age its measure. What oppresses one will exalt the next. Thus it shall be to the end of time.[122]

GOETHE THE MUSICIAN

CHRISTIANA GOETHE
DRAWING BY GOETHE

GOETHE THE MUSICIAN

GOETHE'S attitude towards music has not hitherto received the attention which it deserves, especially in France. The man of letters who is also a musician is a rarity in Latin countries. When men of this type are found, their taste in music is usually so amateurish that it has been supposed that Goethe was cut to the same inadequate measure. Even at his best, Goethe was not considered to be on a higher level than that of a gifted amateur. He was known to be distinguished, refined, and sensitive, but without any technical knowledge, a man who judged musical works according to the impressions which they made upon him; these impressions, at times vivid and penetrating, were largely instinctive, and were often affected by the prevailing fashion of the day. His failure to understand Beethoven was thus set down to an incompetence in an art which was altogether alien to him.

But when we take the trouble to follow Goethe's artistic life from beginning to end, we find that we must abandon this view. From first to last we are struck by the great part which music played in his life.[123]

We know, of course, that he was above all a "visual,"

Zum Sehen geboren,
Zum Schauen bestellt . . .

(Born to see, destined to observe . . .), and that to him the finest harmony was that which was conveyed through his sight. It was he who said so strikingly, "compared with the eye, the ear is a dumb sense" ("*gegen das Auge betrachtet, ist das Ohr ein stummer Sinn*"). Nevertheless, there was no dumb sense in Goethe; every pore, as it were, was open to the beauty of the world, and we can almost say that in his case the ear was a second eye.

As I have already said, his ear was most sensitive. He could not tolerate din; street noises were a torture to him, he had an aversion to the barking of dogs; he avoided the blare of the romantic orchestra, and at the theatre the kettle-drum beats hurt him; he would leave his box in the middle of the performance. We must always bear in mind the extreme sensitiveness of his nerves, the delicate organisms which dominated his mind. His recognition of this heel of Achilles (for he knew all his weaknesses) was largely responsible for his isolation at Weimar, and his fear of large cities.

But do not let us make any mistake. It was noise which he hated; the fulness of rich, pure sound delighted him. He had a fine and powerful bass voice, and liked to hear it.[124] Even at the age of seventy he astounded Mendelssohn by its "tremendous sonority" (*"ungeheurer Klang"*). That voice, had he wished, could have been "heard above the din of ten thousand warriors," the young musician wrote to his sister Fanny. And indeed, when he directed rehearsals at the Weimar Theatre, his commands, thundering forth from his box, filled the whole theatre.[125] When he recited he knew how to use all the registers of his voice.

He had developed this magnificent organ, not only by reading aloud and reciting, but also by singing. As a little child he learnt by heart the tunes of children's songs even before he could understand the meaning of the words, as children mostly do. In Leipzig he sang sentimental duets with the Breitkopf sisters. Never, throughout his life, did he write a *Lied* without humming a melody to it.[126] "Never read, always sing" (*"Nur nicht lesen, immer singen!"*) he wrote in a love poem to Lina, recommending that, in order to read his poems, she sit at the piano and play. Here we have a trait which distinguished him essentially from all our songless poets. Of music he said that it was the "true element from which all poetry is derived and into which all poetry flows," like a river into the sea (*"von der Tonkunst dem wahren Elemente, woher alle Dichtungen entspringen, und wohin sie zurückkehren"*).

Besides singing, he had learned in Frankfurt to play the piano, and in Strasbourg he had studied the 'cello. We read that in 1795, at the age of forty-six, "he played the piano quite well" (*"Er spielt Klavier, und gar nicht schlecht"*).[127] There is, however, reason to believe that after he settled in Weimar (towards the end of 1775) he neglected the piano, except on rare occasions when he used Wieland's instrument. No doubt he did not consider it advisable to be heard at a court of music-lovers in which his fair friend, Frau von Stein, played both the piano and the lute. His privileged position enabled him also to hear music whenever he wished, without having to play himself; he had but to send for the court musicians, who were under his orders.

It is well to remember, however, that music was to him not simply an amusement. It was either an intelligent interest for the mind, a means of soothing, calming, and restoring the spirit, or a source of direct inspiration to creative activity.[128] Thus in 1779 he sent for the musicians "to soothe his soul and set free his spirit" (*"die Seele zu lindern und die Geister zu entbinden"*), while he was writing *Iphigenie.* In 1815-16 he had recourse to music as a help to inspiration while he was writing *Epimenides.* In 1820 he wrote: "I can always work better after I have been listening to music."

There is no doubt that he composed, and that he even wrote in several parts. The following is a curious example:

During the summer of 1813—the year after he met Beethoven—while he was alone in Bohemia and in a depressed frame of mind, he meditated deeply on the immortal words of desperate hope—*In te Domine speravi et non confundar in aeternum.* He set them to music for voices in four parts. The following winter, reading his composition again, he asked Zelter to set the same words to music also in four parts. His obliging friend obeyed. And Goethe, after comparing the two versions, wrote to Zelter (February 23, 1814) that the comparison had thrown a light on his own musical personality; his composition reminded him of Jommelli's style (that wasn't half bad!). He added: "How astonished and pleased we are when we find ourselves unexpectedly on such paths. We become suddenly aware of our own subconscious life" ("*Nachtwandeln*" —literally, "sleepwalking").

But his conception of art was too high to permit the existence of schoolboy compositions; they were written in a language which remained foreign to him, no matter how skilfully he spoke it.

What had been his musical development?

As a child, in Frankfurt, the Italian arias and the French light operas (Sedaine and Favart, Monsigny and Grétry).[129]

In Leipzig, the German *Singspiele* (ballad operas) in which Johann Adam Hiller excelled. But the worthy Hiller, whom Goethe knew personally, was much more than an amiable musician; he was one of the greatest musical instructors in Germany. He had founded a weekly musical journal and had organized excellent symphony and choral concerts (he called them "musical evenings") which later on became the famous *Gewandhaus* concerts. At these performances Hasse's oratorios were given with excellent singers, who roused the enthusiasm of the youthful audiences. Sixty-three years later these memories were still fresh in the mind of the aging Goethe, and he referred to them in two touching poems, written in 1831 on the occasion of the eighty-second birthday of Gertrud Schmehling, who sang under the name of la Mara, the most famous of the soloists who appeared at these Leipzig concerts. Another of the singers, Korona Schröter, was engaged by Goethe, eight years later, to appear in Weimar; they were close friends and seem to have played with fire; it is said that Goethe burnt himself. . . .

During this first period, before Goethe was twenty, the sceptre of music was wielded by Hasse, the great master of pure melody whom even Mozart hardly surpassed. But the influence of Gluck was already becoming apparent. . . . It goes almost without saying that Gluck represented for Goethe one of the loftiest peaks in the art of music,[130] and it was not altogether his fault if the two did not work together. In 1774, when Goethe's period of *Lieder* was in full blossom, after the delightful spring of Strasbourg, he was trying to find a composer who could work hand in hand with him. He asked one of his friends to mention him to Gluck, and she sent some of young Goethe's poems to the old composer. Gluck, unfortunately, was in one of his bad tempers. He refused even to read the poems. He said very angrily that he was very busy and had all the poets he wanted—Marmontel, Sedaine. . . . Alas!

Two years later, in 1776, the rôles were changed; it was Gluck who approached Goethe. They were sad days for Gluck. In April he had lost his adored niece, Nanette Marianna, "the little Chinese girl," the nightingale whose voice was so frail and pathetic. She died at the age of seventeen. Gluck received the terrible news in Paris, on the morning after the first performance of *Alcestis*, which had been a complete failure. He was grief-stricken; nothing mattered any longer; music meant nothing to him; he would not compose again. . . . Yes, he would write one more song in which all his love, all his despair, should cry aloud to the world. He wrote to Klopstock, he wrote to Wieland. Both referred him to Goethe, and it was Wieland who put Gluck's request before his young fellow poet. Goethe was greatly moved; he began to give the matter some thought. But those were days of feverish and troubled anxiety to him. He had just arrived in Weimar, where he was beset by the demands of pride and love. These were the early days of that passionate friendship which was to bring him so many joys, such creative dreams, and such torments. He was the slave of Charlotte von Stein.[131] His thoughts, filled for a while with the grief of the old singer of *Orpheus*, strayed elsewhere; he cast aside the work which he had begun.[132] In vain did Gluck plead. . . .

"My heart is filled with sadness," he wrote to Frau von Stein; "I am writing a poem for Gluck on the death of his niece" (*"Ich wohne in tiefer Trauer über einem Gedicht dass ich für Gluck auf den Tod seiner Nichte machen will"*).[133]

It seems, however, that the plan which he had conceived for this was too vast.[134] He did not find the quiet frame of mind required for such a work, and so he gave it up.[135]

This was not, however, the last time that Goethe and Gluck were in contact. During the years which followed, Gluck was greatly appreciated in Weimar,[136] and Goethe sought from him not only the creative stimulant which he often looked for in the works of musicians, but lessons in dramatic style and declamation.[137] His lovely friend, Korona Schröter, had often sung Gluck to him, and sung it well. Goethe at the time desired to train for his own personal use a composer who should, as it were, complement him. Music, indeed, was to him an integral and necessary part of the lyric and theatrical art with which he was then preoccupied. So he proposed to send Christoph Kayser, whom he had chosen for the purpose, to Gluck. He wrote to Gluck, who at that time was very ill, indeed at death's door, and the latter at once replied, asking to be excused on account of his paralyzed hand (1780).

At this time (1781) Goethe was much interested in Jean-Jacques Rousseau's musical ideas. Goethe's "monodrama" *Proserpina* belongs to a class of play inaugurated by Rousseau's *Pygmalion.*

But there was yet another and more powerful star rising in Goethe's heaven, Handel. Weimar was just then in theatrical matters well ahead of the rest of Germany, and about January-March 1781, the town saw the first performance in Germany of *Alexander's Feast* and of the *Messiah.* This was a great event for Goethe. He followed the rehearsals very closely and, according to his own confession,[138] he acquired "many new ideas on declamation" (*"neue Ideen von Deklamation"*). To Goethe Handel remained one of the gods of Olympus, although he had hardly any further opportunities of hearing his music in the little town.[139] This was probably one of the grounds on which his friendship with Zelter was based.[140] It was a performance of the *Messiah* which had decided the musical career of the young master-mason; it had moved him so deeply that he sobbed bitterly as he walked on foot from Potsdam to Berlin, after the performance (1783). The two friends were haunted by this great work, to such a point that later[141] they decided to write together an immense oratorio which would stand worthily beside the *Messiah.* In letters dating from 1816, Goethe sketched out the basic ideas of the plan:

"The two ideas: Necessity and Liberty. . . . In this circle everything is to be found in which man is interested. . . ."

The work was to begin with the thunder on Mount Sinai, the "Thou shalt" (*"Du sollst"*), and end with Christ's resurrection, and the "Thou shalt be" (*"Du wirst"*).

It has been justly pointed out that although this plan so enthusiastically conceived did not mature, the second *Faust* profited by several of its inspirations; the Epilogue in Heaven is its direct result. Who would ever have thought that *Faust,* in this magnificent peroration, is the indirect heir of Handel?

We shall see later how the exultant and illuminating art of Handel affected Goethe's imperious tastes in religious music. There was, in fact, a preëstablished harmony between him and this form of art.

As he grew old, he felt an irresistible desire to rejuvenate his aging mind in this fountain of energy. In the spring of 1824 an essay by Rochlitz on the *Messiah* rekindled the fire of his imagination. He wrote to Zelter he imbibed with delight Handel's *Geistesgewalt* ("Gigantic Spiritual Power"). If anything could have persuaded him to emerge from his retreat in Weimar and go to Berlin, it was Zelter's great orchestral and choral performances, which reawakened in Germany the all-embracing spirit of Handel and Bach. Goethe eagerly read Zelter's letters on this subject; by means of them he heard the performances almost as perfectly as we would hear them by wireless.

"It is," he once said, "as if I heard at a distance the sound of the sea" (*"Es ist mir als wenn ich von ferne das Meer brausen hörte"*).

There is a close analogy between these words and Beethoven's remark on hearing Bach's music: "His name should not be brook (Bach), but sea . . ." (*"Nicht Bach sondern Meer sollte er heissen wegen seines unendlichen, unausschöpfbaren Reichtums von Tonkombinationen und Harmonien"*).[142]

Goethe was not only overwhelmed by these musical immensities; he also admired the architectural beauty of the oratorios. During the last three years of his life he never tired of studying the construction of the *Messiah, Samson,* and *Judas Maccabaeus* (1829-32).

Towards the close of the year 1785 another star began to shine in his firmament—Mozart. Goethe then heard, for the first time, the opera *Il Seraglio,* in Weimar. He was delighted with it. But this opera was a serious blow to him, for just then he and Kayser were making great efforts to evolve a form of comedy with music. Suddenly, at a single stroke, Mozart wiped out all they had done, realized all they had hoped to achieve, and surpassed their utmost ambitions. Goethe, however, was not so narrow-minded as to bear him any ill-will.[143] From the day on which Goethe became the director of the Weimar theatre, Mozart reigned supreme, and his reign endured.

We must not forget that, for twenty-six years, from May, 1791, to April, 1817, the climax of his life, Goethe undertook a task which to us seems ungrateful and out of all proportion to his genius, namely, the direction of a provincial theatre where not only plays, but operas also, were given.[144] He took this work very seriously, especially until 1808, when the perpetual quarrels incited by the prima-donna Karolina Jagemann, who was the recognized mistress of the duke, and who used her position to impose her will on the management of the theatre, caused him the utmost disgust. But during the long period of his direction, 600 pieces were performed, of which 104 were operas, and 31 *Singspiele* (ballad operas). Mozart's works easily held the first place. When, in 1795, Goethe summed up the work of the theatre during its first ten years, he found that not one work had been given more than twelve performances, except *The Magic*

Flute with twenty-two, and *Il Seraglio* with twenty-five performances. Twenty years later, the total number of performances of Mozart's operas under Goethe's direction were: 82 of *The Magic Flute*,[145] 68 of *Don Juan*, 49 of *Il Seraglio*, 33 of *Così fan Tutte*, 28 of *Titus*, and 19 of *The Marriage of Figaro*, which, strangely enough, was in Weimar always the least successful of Mozart's works. Until the advent of Schiller's dramas, Mozart remained the first favourite; after Schiller's death, opera again outweighed drama. Goethe's best pieces, *Faust, Tasso, Iphigenie, Götz von Berlichingen*, were played only long after they were written and on rare occasions. More frequently we find his lighter works, his *Singspiele*, of which even the most popular, *Jery und Bätely,* was given 24 times only. Mozart's supremacy in this theatre is therefore incontestable.

That Goethe agreed with the public verdict is proved by a famous letter to Schiller. The latter had expressed to his friend the great hopes which he had founded on opera; he was even of the opinion that "just as once upon a time tragedy was evolved from the choruses of the ancient feasts of Bacchus, it would again emerge from opera, but in a nobler form," because opera was free from the slavish imitation of nature, and in it art had "free play." Goethe replied: "You could have seen your expectation of the future of opera realized to a high degree in *Don Juan.* But this work remains unique, and with Mozart's death all hope of hearing anything like it is lost."

He expressed the same regret towards the end of his life,[146] when he deplored with Eckermann, in 1829, that he could find no suitable music for *Faust.* "It is quite impossible," said Goethe. "The music would have to be in the character of *Don Juan.* Mozart should have composed it."[147]

It is said that the last songs which Goethe heard were melodies from *Don Juan,* which his grandson Walther sang him on the evening of March 10th.[148]

Among the other masters of the lyric theatre whose works were most frequently performed in Weimar under Goethe's direction we find, during the early days, Dittersdorf, Benda, Paesiello, Cimarosa, Monsigny, Dalayrac, Gretry, Salieri, and Sarti.[149] After 1800, Cherubini, Méhul, Boïeldieu. After 1810, Paer, Simon Mayr, and Spontini. Weber made his appearance in 1814 with *Silvana,* Beethoven's *Egmont* was given in 1812-14, and his *Fidelio* in 1816. Then came Rossini's period of triumphs: *Semiramis, La Gazza Ladra, The Siege of Corinth,* later *William*

Tell and *Moses.* The only works which rivalled his were those of Spontini, for whom Goethe showed much consideration, and whom he treated as Rossini's equal, and Weber's *Freischütz.* Finally there was Auber. Goethe, who at that time did not visit the theatre frequently, heard, in 1824, *Euryanthe* and *Freischütz, Fernando Cortez, Tancredi, The Marriage of Figaro*; in 1826 the *Barber of Seville*; in 1827 *La Gazza Ladra*; in 1828 *La Dame Blanche* and *The Mason*; in 1829 *Oberon*, which aggravated him. This was the last.

Dramatic music was not sufficient for Goethe. He also liked sacred music on a large scale, and chamber music.

As far as the first was concerned, the resources available in Weimar were very meagre. During the finest epoch, that of Schiller and Herder, all that was given in the course of ten years were three or four oratorios by Haydn and Graun. The difficulty was that Herder, the general superintendent of schools and churches, and Goethe, the director of the theatre, were compelled by lack of resources to compete for the services of choristers. Herder complained, not without reason, that Goethe deprived him of the seminarist choir; but Goethe was forced to take this step in order to carry on his opera house.

The chamber music consisted principally of concerts by virtuosi. Goethe, however, was not satisfied. His lifelong wish, as he expressed it in *Wilhelm Meister*, was that music should form part of our daily life. His dream was a private choir, and in September, 1807, he carried his plan into effect. The times were ripe for meditation and the culture of the arts. Germany's defeat, after the battle of Jena, forced the country to turn to its own spiritual resources. Bode has pointed out how the different classes of society and the different provinces of the *Vaterland* were brought closer together. Everybody felt, as never before and never afterwards, the need of spiritual communion in their most sacred emotions, in art and in thought.

Goethe's prestige was growing rapidly during those years; he was well aware that "*noblesse oblige*" would prevent him from accepting any benefit which would not, at the same time, prove of service to those who surrounded him, and through them, Weimar setting the example, to the whole of Germany. Two months after the foundation of his private choir he presented it to a circle of chosen friends, and a month later to the court; still later (February 22, 1810) to the whole town.

This choir, which had very modest beginnings, was really a choral society (a four-part chorus). The young violinist and composer, Karl Eberwein, soon became the conductor. The repertoire, which increased rapidly, consisted mainly of the great Italian and German sacred music: Jommelli, Joseph Haydn, Mozart, Fasch, Salieri, Ferrari (offertories, motets, canons, hymns), as well as *Lieder* by Zelter, Reichardt, and Eberwein. Even masses and fragments of oratorios were introduced. Of course Goethe's personal influence was felt much more in the rendering of the *Lieder* and the humorous compositions, because there the poet and theatrical producer insisted on his rights; it was he who decided on the *tempi* and the expression.

But in the execution of both kinds of music, sacred or secular, there was one inexorable law which Goethe imposed on his musicians and which governed the choice of his programs; he would have none of the tendency, then so common in Germany, to whining, to religious lamentations and love laments, to what he called "graveyard music." Though the particular circumstances of that period would have admitted, or even prompted, melancholy, this energetic man forbade its expression. He cursed the weeping-willow poets who had opened the flood-gates of this mournful inundation, among them Matthisson and Tiedge, both friends of Beethoven. I am not sure that the mere mention of the subject did not set him against the immortal song-cycle, *"An die ferne Geliebte"* ("To the distant beloved"), which his Zuleika, Marianna von Willemer, recommended so strongly to him. In the course of a journey in 1817 he heard a melancholy love song, "I have loved and love no more; I have laughed and laugh no more . . ."; he was furious and wrote at his hotel table:

"I have loved, and now I begin to love more than ever. . . . Today as yesterday, the stars are shining. Avoid as you would the plague those whose heads are bowed in woe. Live always as if life were just beginning!" (*"und lebe dir immer von vorne"*)!

This, then, was another trait, one of the best, which he shared with Zelter, who bore so many troubles on his shoulders and shook them off so cheerily.

What Goethe demanded both of sacred and of secular music was that it should set free the joy of living, moral confidence, whole-hearted energy, and above all, the impulse of reason; it should encourage the spirit of clearness of thought, the sense of the eternal, contempt for pettiness and nothingness. In that he is blood brother to Handel. What would not these two together have done, the Apollo of Weimar and the English Hercules? This preference was undoubtedly detrimental to Beethoven, yet he would have been the first to approve of it. It was not Beethoven's fault if he did not follow the same road as Handel. It was an ideal which greatly attracted him, but which the tormented soul of the man prevented his attaining. Besides, let us make no mistake; for Goethe, too, Handel represented an ideal, whose faculty for abundant joyousness in music and whose serene mind attracted him all the more because he himself did not possess them, as he told his friend Councillor von Müller. He compared himself to Napoleon and contrasted himself with him: Napoleon loved only tender and melancholy music because these qualities were opposed and complementary to his own character. Goethe said that soft and sentimental melodies depressed him: "I need lively (*frische*) and energetic music to grip and uplift me. Napoleon, who was a tyrant, needed softness in music. I, for the very reason that I am not a tyrant, love lively, gay, merry (*rauschende, lebhafte, heitere*) music. Man aspires always to be what he is not."[150] Should we therefore be justified in saying that in Beethoven he avoided what he himself was . . . what he himself did not desire to be? . . .

In his choir, in his home, he cultivated gay secular music, folksong especially, and virile sacred music. He was also very fond of string quartets; it was, indeed, the form of instrumental music he liked best. Here again he agreed with Beethoven whose real and essential nature found expression from beginning to end in the string quartet . . . The quadriga suited Apollo . . . What Goethe derived above all from this form of music was a pleasure founded on reason:

"I hear," he wrote to Zelter, "four people of good sense discoursing together; I have the feeling that I learn something from what they are saying, and I become acquainted with the individuality of each of them."[151]

He disliked, however, the violent shocks which the new instrumental music afforded. He must have conceived it as an attack upon the liberty of the mind, which is thus surprised and brutally violated. All that the mind could not grasp thoroughly, all that he summed up in the word *meteorisches* (of meteoric quality), was suspect, even antagonistic to him. Very probably, under this term he condemned, or at least segregated, Weber's operas and some of Beethoven's symphonies, the feasts of Dionysus, the orgies, the hurricanes, as he called them.

His private choir lasted about seven or eight years only. As in the theatre, he succumbed to the poison of intrigue, to the petty quarrels of a vain and bickering horde whose habits Goethe so well knew (he describes them in masterly fashion in *Wilhelm Meister*), but who attracted him, nevertheless. After 1814 he kept only two or three of his singers, who had become his personal friends.

At this moment, just as the springs of his musical knowledge seemed to fail, his horizon was suddenly widened enormously by his intercourse with Bach.

The Bachs were well known in Weimar where they had neighbours and relatives. John Sebastian came to Weimar on two occasions, once in 1703 for a few months and then in 1708 for nine months, as organist and *Kapellmeister*. His Weimar pupils maintained his traditions in that town for half a century.[152] Moreover, the dowager duchess, who came from Brunswick and was a good musician, had studied under John Ernest Bach, of Eisenach, who had followed her to Weimar. It is very probable that she often played John Sebastian's works to Goethe.

Goethe must also have met many other admirers of John Sebastian, for there were many of them in those days: there was, for instance, young Count Wolf Baudissin who used to say that he was ready to die for Bach, much to Goethe's disgust.[153] Goethe's friend Rochlitz, the historian of music, had in 1800 reminded the all-too-forgetful German people that the last surviving daughter of Bach was living in utter poverty, and had asked the public to send donations for her: Beethoven was a warm supporter of this charitable appeal. Lastly Zelter had in 1810 given short lectures to Goethe on John Sebastian and his great rivals or forerunners. Goethe, therefore, was well informed of Bach's importance, and of his place in the evolution of music.

But the direct experience of Bach's music and the definite impression it left on him he owed to his friend the inspector of Berka Spa near Weimar, Johann Heinrich Friedrich Schütz. This merry little fat man with his rubicund face, and his top-hat set askew on his head, was a passionate admirer of Bach. He had bought bundles of manuscript music from John Sebastian's last pupil, Kittell of Erfurt. This music he played to Goethe, who was at once greatly impressed and remained so to the end of his days, which shows that his musical disposition was essentially serious. He was never tired of hearing the "Well-tempered Clavichord" and was always asking Schütz to play him the preludes and fugues. He likened them to "brilliant mathematical works, the themes of which are so simple and the poetical results are so magnificent."[154] From that time Schütz and Goethe met frequently. Either one or the other would pay a visit to his friend in the neighbouring town. The piano would at once be opened, and inspired reason, in a never-ending stream of music, would pour forth. In 1818 Goethe had this music played to him for three or four hours a day for three whole weeks. Referring to the perfect sense of repose which this gave him, he used to say, "I go to bed, and Schütz plays me Sebastian."

Schütz sometimes played well into the night. Goethe, Zelter, and he often gave one another Bach's music as presents, his chorales, for instance, and the "Well-tempered Clavichord." It must also be mentioned to Zelter's great credit that he was the first to revive the *Passion according to St. Matthew.* He conducted it in Berlin with his *Singakademie*, his regiment, as he called it, with the support of young Mendelssohn.[155] Zelter's letters to Goethe frequently mentioned the wonderful wealth of organ music which he had introduced.[156] And Goethe's whole being vibrated in unison with this mighty ocean, with its roar heard from afar.[157]

Since for Goethe there was no musical enjoyment in which reason did not share, his letters to Zelter frequently show his scientific interest in Bach. Now he is studying the second volume of Rochlitz's essays *On Bach's Compositions for the Keyboard* (1825); now he questions Zelter eagerly on the Couperins, and their alleged influence on John Sebastian (1827).

His anthropocentric genius is always seeking the principles of art and science in the laws which govern the human body and its sensibilities.[158] In his study of the relations of body and mind in music, he points out the importance, as shown in Bach, of the foot and of the hand in organ-playing.[159]

Goethe saw far beyond John Sebastian and that preclassic age of which the men of letters and even the musicians of his day knew so little. He was well acquainted with the vocal polyphony of the sixteenth century. He had discovered its beauty during his stay in Rome in Lent, 1788, at the Sistine Chapel, and his friend Christoph Kayser had helped him to understand it. They had listened together assiduously to the *a cappella* works by Palestrina, Morales, and Allegri. In Milan they had studied the Ambrosian chants.

Goethe had also commissioned Kayser to make researches into ancient music, because his intuition told him that here was to be found the source of Christian chants.[160] Later, when at Weimar Goethe attended the Easter church services which were sung by the Greek choir of the hereditary princes, he was struck by the close relation between the Russian hymns and the Sistine chants, and he asked Zelter to tell him something of the origin of old Byzantine music.[161] But Zelter's classical erudition was so poor that he did not even know the meaning of the word "Byzantine."[162]

In Rochlitz he would have found a musical guide of much greater culture. But, in spite of his long connection with him, it seems as if Goethe feared to offend his old friend Zelter if he summoned Rochlitz to Weimar.[163] However, he read Rochlitz's books, and especially during the latter part of his life, when he went out less, he studied musical history assiduously.[164]

All this, however, did not satisfy his intellectual hunger. In music, as in all other branches of knowledge, his mind sought to deduce a scientific theory from his experiences and the facts which came to his knowledge. He sought to establish a *Tonlehre* (Theory of Musical Sounds) as a parallel to his *Farbenlehre* (Colour Theory). His aim was the discovery, in the multiplicity of phenomena, of the primitive and central Unit, *"So muss das alles eins werden, alles aus Einem entspringen und zu Einem zurückkehren . . .* (1810) ("So everything must become one, everything must issue from one source, and must revert to it").

He found some eminent associates with whom to discuss the problem of natural science in music: the mathematician, Johann Friedrich Christian Verneburg of Eisenach (about 1808-11), and the famous specialist in acoustics, Ernst Chladni of Wittenberg (between 1803 and 1816), whom he liked for his independence of academic science. But his usual colleagues in these discussions were his Zelter, who recited to him such science as he had learnt by heart and whose schoolboy creeds Goethe mercilessly crushed, and an intelligent young man, Christian Schlosser; Goethe intended to make the latter his musical secretary, to write, in accordance with the lines laid down by the master, the *Tonlehre*, which he proposed to publish. Schlosser, however, was not interested in this. Lacking his collaboration, Goethe was unable to carry out his plan, but the scheme was never abandoned.[165] So keen was his interest in it, that, as late as the year 1827, he had the main lines of his *Tonlehre* written out elaborately on a large sheet, which he framed and hung in his bedroom. Although, according to his own admission, he never got beyond the mere skeleton of this science, his theories are considered worthy of discussion by some authoritative writers on music of our present day. Hans Joachim Moser published a monograph on *Goethe und die Musikalische Akustik,*[166] and Hugo Riemann expressed his approval of Goethe's theories.

The problem which interested Goethe particularly, and at which he worked till the eve of his death[167] was that of the minor mode. He discussed it with Zelter in 1808, 1810, and 1821, and with Schlosser in 1814-15. Zelter's replies did not satisfy him at all, for Zelter had recourse to explanations based on the physics of music—*i.e.*, the divisions of the string. The minor third, according to him, was not a spontaneous manifestation of nature, but a product of art, derived from the major third. Goethe disagreed entirely. It is human nature, he said, which is the source of the musical universe (*Tonwelt*). It is in this direction that we must search, and not experiment with artificial instruments such as are used for mathematical tests. "What indeed is a string and its mechanical divisions, compared with the musician's ear? We can go further and say, What are natural phenomena compared with the man who must first master and modify them all, in order to be able, in a certain degree, to assimilate them?"[168]

His powerful subjectivism eagerly seized upon Schlosser's suggestion, that the two modes, major and minor, are two different manifestations of the same single *Tonmonade*—the living unit of sound. "If the *Tonmonade* expands, the result is the major mode, if it contracts, then the minor mode is produced."

The centre of the monad is formed by the deepest sound, and the periphery by the highest. But Goethe and Schlosser did not agree on the æsthetic and intellectual value of the two modes. Schlosser, with a strong inclination towards romantic religiosity, was of the opinion that music's centre of gravity was to be found in the melancholy of the soul which tends to introspection, and withdraws from outside influences; the minor mode to him was the most intimate expression of the human heart in its aspiration towards the infinite. Goethe protested against this; he would not allow that sadness is the centre of the soul and of art. He was willing to admit that human nature has a double tendency. On the one hand it seeks the objective, demands activity, and claims external things; on the other it seeks the subjective, demands concentration, and claims those things which are within itself. The major mode was the expression of all that excited, exalted, and propelled the soul towards the outer world. The minor mode was, perhaps, the mode of concentration. But concentration was in no sense synonymous with sadness. No, a thousand times no! What sadness could there be in a polonaise that was in a minor key? These were popular dances, and those who joined in them did so with an ardent desire to commingle soul and body. Was this sadness or voluptuousness?[169] (How fine it is to watch the vigorous old man brush aside with a sweep of his hand all the melancholy of the effeminate romanticism which was to come!)

But there is another example, and a much more interesting one. I mean the *Marseillaise*, that *Marseillaise* which Beethoven, in some inexplicable way, never seems to have noticed and of which I cannot discover a single trace in his work. How utterly unaware he was of it is shown by the fact that, as late as 1813, he introduced the grotesque Malbrouck march in his *Battle of Vittoria* to represent his idea of the French.[170]

Goethe had heard it on the battle field of the Argonne, at Valmy and in Mainz, and he remained under its stimulating influence for the whole of his life. It is interesting to know that what impressed him most, and what he remembered best, was the sombre and menacing minor, the shadow, not the light. But for him this shadow had nothing in common with a depression of the spirit. It was, on the contrary, an explosion of avenging fury. . . .

"I know nothing more terrible than military music in a minor key. Here the two extremes clash, and wound the heart instead of stunning it. The most remarkable example of this is the *Marseillaise*."

"Dagegen ich nie etwas schrecklicheres gekannt habe als einen kriegerischen Marsch aus dem Mollton. Hier wirken die beiden Pole innerlich gegeneinander und

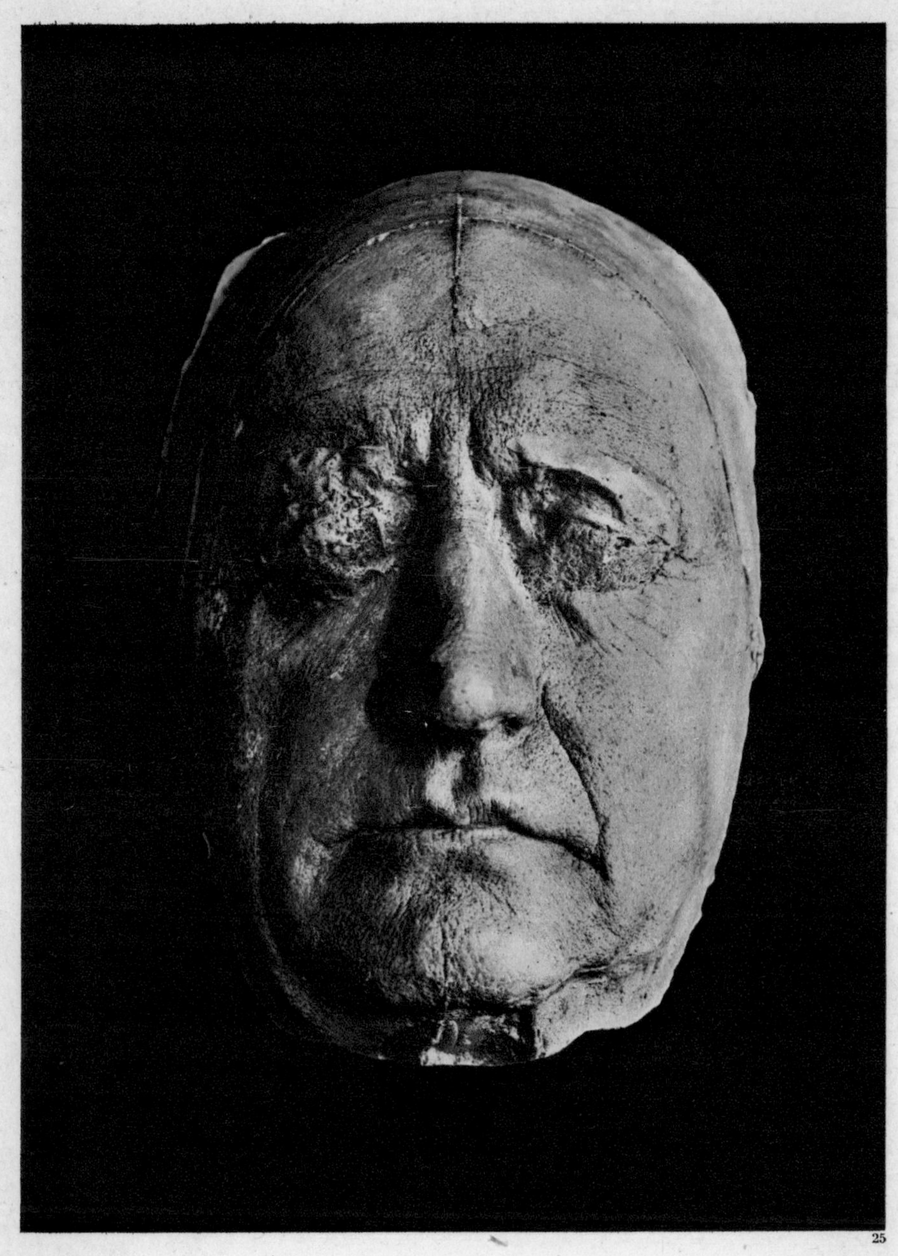

25

26

27

quetschen das Herz, anstatt es zu indifferenzieren. Das eminenteste Beispiel gibt uns der Marseiller Marsch."[171]

We see then how wide and prolonged Goethe's musical experience had been; he had played himself, he had heard a great variety of musical performances, he had meditated upon music, he had studied its history and science. What then were his shortcomings, what was there in the music of the time which escaped him?

Intellectually, very little indeed. The new tendencies which were working in were felt by him as well as by others. In June, 1805, when he was writing a commentary on *Le Neveu de Rameau*, he distinguished between two musical schools—the Italian, essentially vocal and melodic, and the German, instrumental and harmonic—and he longed for the advent of the master, who, uniting the two, should introduce into instrumental music the forces of sentiment (*Gemütskräfte*).[172]

He was right, and his conclusion should have been, "The master has come . . . he is Beethoven." But at that time Goethe had not yet heard any of his music.[173]

Did Goethe lay down any limits to the expressive and descriptive powers of the art of sound? No; when in 1818 Adalbert Schoepke asked him, "What are the limits of expression in music?" Goethe answered, "It is the great and noble privilege of music to create a mood within us without using ordinary exterior means for the purpose" (*"Das Innere in Stimmung zu setzen, ohne die gemeinen äusseren Mittel zu brauchen, ist der Musik grosses und edles Vorrecht"*).

These are exactly Beethoven's principles, *"Mehr Ausdruck der Empfindung als Mahlerei"* (rather an expression of feelings than a pictorial representation). More than that, Goethe recognized that music is privileged to go further than reason, and to penetrate regions for ever closed to speech and analytic intelligence. In his conversations with Eckermann on "demoniacal matters" (*"das Dämonische"*) he referred to the unconscious or subconscious poetry, for the comprehension of which intelligence and reason prove insufficient, and continued:

"The same applies, in the highest degree to music, because music occupies so lofty a plane that reason cannot approach it; from music emanates an influence which dominates all, an influence of which no man may give an account" (*"Desgleichen ist es in der Musik im höchsten Grade, denn sie steht so hoch dass kein Verstand ihr beikommen kann, und es geht von ihr eine Wirkung aus, die Alles beherrscht und von der Niemand im Stande ist sich Rechenschaft zu geben"*).[174]

Is this not a confirmation of the exalted profession of faith which Beethoven made to Bettina:[175]

"Music is the single, the immaterial entry into a higher world of knowledge which envelops man but which he cannot understand."

It is indeed much that this master of intelligence, the great Goethe, should at the close of his life recognize the sovereign rights of musical intuition.

Would it then not have been possible for Beethoven and Goethe to agree? What was the stumbling-block to Goethe's musical understanding? As far as intellectual understanding is concerned, there was none. But his physiological tolerance failed him when those natural limits were reached which advanced age imposes on organic sensitiveness. It was asking too much of a man of the time of Cimarosa, Haydn, and Mozart to share the feelings of the age of Weber, Schubert, and Berlioz.[176] Is any one of us capable of a complete rejuvenation after half a century of life? The only new musical genius whom Goethe could normally have adopted and incorporated in himself, during the cycle of his life, was Beethoven. I have tried to explain the reason why he failed to do so.

Certainly the greatness and the achievements of Weber, Schubert, and Berlioz escaped him. It is of interest, then, to examine more closely certain of these failures in understanding, particularly in the case of Schubert.

Schubert, in 1814, at the age of seventeen, had made his first appearance and during the following year had set to music some of Goethe's *Lieder*; in 1816 he composed his splendid *Erl King*, and asked the poet, through his friend Spaun, for permission to dedicate this work to him. Goethe did not reply; he had not read it, for his time was entirely taken up with other matters. And who was there to sing it to him? Who knew the name of "Schubert" in 1815?

His attitude of refusal was more serious when, ten years later, on June 16, 1825, Goethe received on the same day a quartet by Mendelssohn and the wonderful melody, *An Schwager Kronos*, and two other songs, *An Mignon* and *Ganymed*, by Schubert, with a very respectful dedication to himself. Goethe mentioned with satisfaction the gift from Mendelssohn, whom he liked personally, but he never replied to Schubert. Is there any excuse for this? Weimar's best musician, Hummel, "discovered" Schubert only in 1827; Marianna von Willemer, as always well in advance of others, had been greatly impressed by the *Lieder* from the *Divan* and had mentioned them to Goethe; she had forgotten only one detail in her letter, the composer's name!

There is, however, proof that between 1825 and 1830 Goethe heard some of Schubert's most famous *Lieder*, and that his first attitude was strong disapproval. One of the works was the *Erl King.* Can we wonder? Goethe naturally judged it from the poet's point of view.[177] He had written the poem as the simple story told by a poor washerwoman, who hums it, almost without giving a thought to the words; the song weaves about her and her work an atmosphere of popular fantasy. . . . Goethe was now presented with a melodramatic piece full of theatrical effects—raging tempests and so on. . . . He was annoyed with the lightning flashes, and the rolling thunder, so out of all proportion to his simple idyll. He saw in the song merely lack of intelligence and exaggeration. He shrugged his shoulders. . . . We can hear Zelter scoffing at Beethoven, "Those people use the club of Hercules to kill a fly!"

If there was one vice in art which Goethe could not tolerate, it was the *"Non erat is locus"* ("Out of place").

But though he grumbled to his heart's content at the liberty which the composer had taken with his work, could he not have risen above it and been artist enough to see the beauty of the music, even if its effect differed from his own conception?

He did recognize it. When, on April 24, 1830, Wilhelmine Schröder-Devrient came to his house and sang the *Erl King*, he was moved to the very fibres of his being, and he was noble enough to make his *mea culpa* to the spirit of Schubert. He said: "I had already heard this song, and it meant nothing to me. But sung like this, it conjures up a great picture before my eyes." And he kissed the forehead of the inspiring singer.

Similarly, a month later (May 25) he had at last to bow his head, whether he liked it or not, before the elemental force of the C Minor Symphony, which Mendelssohn unrolled before him.

At the age of eighty-one he had still sufficient vigour to cross the mighty ravine which Beethoven and Schubert had cleft, as it were, in the road of his musical appreciation. Is this not an achievement? None could say that in him old age had frozen the stream of life. Which of us at his age would keep so open a mind and display such energy?

Of Berlioz Goethe knew nothing. Zelter's abominable letter, in which he poured a stream of the vilest invective on Berlioz's *Eight Scenes from Faust*, had disgusted him for ever with this style of composition (June, 1829).

In conclusion, Weber. Here Goethe's lack of appreciation was due fundamentally to the personal antipathy of which I have already written, and to the old man's intolerance of the din of brasses and percussion instruments which were then a novel feature of orchestration. Even Spontini, whom Goethe held in particularly high esteem, upset him with his noisy orchestration of his *Vestale.* "This noise," he told Christian Lobe, "quickly tires me" (*mich bald ermüdet*). To which Lobe replied that one got used to it as one got used to Mozart, who at first proved very tiring.

"But there must be a limit," Goethe went on, "beyond which one cannot go without injury to the ear."

"No doubt there is," replied the young man. "But the fact that most people can now listen to Spontini, seems to prove that this limit has not yet been reached."

And Goethe, faced with the fact, admitted that it might be so (*"Es mag sein"*).

But this was in truth the whole point, and this was the real reason of the *dignus intrare*, which he granted, or refused, to new works of art, "There must be a limit. . . ." Yes. But where is it? Nothing is more natural than that in 1829 the aged Goethe and his old friend Zelter should have found that the new music had exceeded this limit, not only in the means which it employed, but also in its portrayal of emotion.

"It exceeds the level of human sensibility. We can no longer follow it either in thought or action." (*"Alles ist jetzt ultra. Alles transzendiert unaufhaltsam an Denken und Tun . . ."*).

Just as our pre-war generation judges the youth of today, so Goethe deplored that, long before maturity, the younger generation had been shaken to the roots, "that the whirlwind of the times had carried it away" before quiet and meditation had had time to restore to it balance of personality. The year 1830, as Goethe saw it, was already given over to the turmoil of discordance and erratic action for which we blame—or for which we praise—the year 1930. In reality it is the periodical conflict of two successive stages of sensitiveness, a conflict which follows unceasingly a curve of regular progression, without, however, passing certain limits; for, as the curve rises, the lower parts gradually vanish, the sensitiveness of former periods disappears; it is, as it were, a new keyboard, which has the same number of octaves as the old. But, while the structure remains the same, the mentality which is housed in it shifts from one level to another. And as organic tolerance thus moves with the times, those who live longer than the normal span of life are bound to suffer from variations in the rhythm and in the intensity of their sensations. They cannot acclimatize themselves to the new conditions.

The onward march of the generations is strictly normal. Goethe at the beginning of his artistic career had heard in 1763 the playing of the child Mozart. Just before his death he had listened to little Clara Wieck (October 4 and 5, 1831), who was to become Schumann's wife and muse.[178] He had withstood with a magnificent strength the strain induced by the conflict of two epochs so different in character.

Our survey of Goethe's musical disposition would be far from complete if we merely considered its passive side—hearing and understanding. A powerful nature, a mind such as his, receives nothing without restoring it enriched and ennobled. Wherever Goethe passed, he created.

As, however, he was not a musician by profession, but a poet, it is interesting to discover what traces music has left in his poetic creations.

The first trace is his keen desire to write libretti: the importance which Goethe attributes to this, and the tenacity with which he persevered in it, rather surprises us. This inclination of his may almost be compared to the great passion which Ingres, the famous painter, had for his violin.[179] Many hours, many days were given to this work; his efforts and his researches deserved a nobler object and a more striking success.

Goethe sketched or attempted one form of musical play after the other. In 1766, in early youth, he wrote a libretto for an Italian operetta, *La Sposa Rapita.*[180] Then followed the German *Singspiel* (ballad opera), or the *Lustspiel* (prose comedy), to which he added arias and *Lieder*; in 1773-74 he wrote his *Erwin und Elmire*, for which Johann Andreas Offenbach composed the score. Later in life, as we have seen, he was considering the possibility of a dramatic-musical collaboration with Gluck, and when the old man did not receive him kindly he chose a young and gifted musical friend, Christoph Kayser, whom he hoped to shape in accordance with his views. At the same time, with his friend, Korona Schröter, he mastered the art of the ballet and devised new forms (1782). During the first period of his life at Weimar everything that he wrote was intended for accompaniment by instrumental or vocal music. A good example of this is his *Proserpina*, a monodrama, spoken to music, after the style of Rousseau (1776). Another example is his *Lila*, a fairy opera. It was then that he studied Handel's and Gluck's declamatory style. His plans, however, could not be fully carried out in Weimar, because he lacked the coöperation of a competent musician.

In 1779-80 he went with his grand duke to Switzerland. His chief motive for going was the hope of meeting Kayser again, who had settled in Zürich, and of writing with him a *Singspiel* on a Swiss subject. This was *Jery und Bätely.* His letters to Kayser give us a very clear definition of the music which he wanted. This time it was Quinault who gave orders to Lulli.* For this play Goethe wanted three distinct kinds of music:

1. Folk songs.
2. Emotional airs.
3. Music to accompany dialogue, adapted to the miming of the actors.

This dialogue must preserve a unity of style, which should be based, if possible, on a principal theme and developed by modulations, modes and rhythms, but it should never lose its logical sense and its outline, which must be simple and clear. "The dialogue must be like a smooth golden ring, in which the airs and *Lieder* are set like precious stones" (*"Der Dialog muss wie ein glatter goldener Ring sein, auf dem Arien und Lieder wie Edelgesteine aufsitzen"*).[181]

* TRANSLATOR'S NOTE.—Lulli, the court musician of Louis XIV, was accustomed to prescribe to Quinault, a poet of merit, the subject and treatment of the libretti which he required for his operas.

The composer, so Goethe maintained, must absorb thoroughly the character of the piece. This general character should dictate the style of all the melodies and accompaniments. The orchestra should be quite small, and the accompaniment not overpowering. "The riches of music lie in discretion. A composer who knows his work can do more with two violins, a viola, and a bass, than others with a whole orchestra." The wood-wind should be what spice is to a dish. The instruments should be used one by one: now the flute, now the oboe, now the bassoon. In this way the purity of the music will give the greater pleasure. Most modern composers, on the contrary, serve everything together, with the result that fish and meat, whether roasted or boiled, taste the same.[182]

Goethe, however, was then only at the beginning of his misunderstandings with Kayser. The latter worked so slowly at his composition, that Goethe had to take the play from him and give it to another composer, the nobleman in charge of the amusements at the Court of Weimar. Finally he lost all interest in the matter.

Nevertheless, Goethe did not give up hope of Kayser. He had him invited to Weimar. In vain did he try to make a man of the world of him, in vain did he persuade him to take to heart the last teachings of Gluck, just before the latter's death. In vain—all in vain! Yet in 1783 he wrote the *libretti* for five ballad operas (*Singspiele*).[183]

Some time afterwards he heard a good Italian company and at once abandoned the hybrid form of spoken dialogue mixed with comic-opera songs, and decided to write, still with Kayser's coöperation, short operettas, entirely sung, and *opera buffa.* For five years, from 1784 to 1789, he worked at an operetta, with three characters—Scapin, Scapine, and the doctor—*"Scherz, List und Rache"* ("Jest, Cunning, and Vengeance"). On this subject he corresponded with Kayser almost as widely as he corresponded with Schiller on the subject of *Wilhelm Meister.* All the evidence goes to show that he attached far greater importance to the subject than it really deserved. He desired to create in Germany a new kind of dramatic-musical art, and he wanted the first production of the kind to be a masterpiece. But apart from the fact that he had no adequate helper and had to do practically the whole of the musician's work as well as his own, it was an art of which he knew nothing; he had to learn as he worked—*Fit fabricando faber.* Unfortunately, the knowledge which he gathered while working was acquired too late: it showed him his errors only after they had been committed. When he saw Mozart's *Il Seraglio,* in 1785, he realized his weak points, but too late. Mozart, without

Goethe's preliminary process of thought, but from sheer instinct, from the impulse of genius, had given the German theatre a comedy with music, full of feeling, sparkling with joy, like the rain and sunshine of a lovely day in spring. Thus Goethe discovered the utter sterility of the intellectual perfection which he had conceived in a work so deeply—all too deeply—thought out. There were only three characters in the four acts, all three of them rogues. He now decided to have seven characters and to give emotion a large part in the plot. But a casting which is almost cold cannot be remoulded; Kayser had already shaped himself in the first mould, had lost all elasticity, and could not follow the constant changes of his great collaborator's mind. The final result was an unheard-of waste of time, and an enormous amount of work expended for no result. In autumn, 1789, Goethe, honest as always, surveyed his past efforts and admitted, "All this tremendous work is lost" (*"Geht die ungeheure Arbeit verloren"*).[184]

Of these ruins the most enduring relic is perhaps his correspondence with Kayser, in which we find a powerful and striking æsthetic idea of the theatre. Goethe insisted that everything in this work should be "*saltatio*,"[185] which he described to Kayser as a continuous melodic and rhythmic movement. He mentioned this repeatedly:

"My highest conception of drama is action without interruption" (*"Mein höchster Begriff vom Drama ist rastlose Handlung"*).

Here again Goethe nearly went too far in his conception of intellectual perfection. But he pulled himself up. His knowledge of the psychology of the public, all the keener for his experience of the theatre and of actors, showed him that it was impossible to realize such a plan. Human nature would not lend itself to it. Goethe came to the conclusion that repose must alternate with movement, and that the climax of movement and of sound must be reserved for the end of the piece. It was what the masters of Italian farcical opera (*opera buffa*) had already done by instinct.

Goethe also gave much time to the careful study of poetical rhythm in comedy set to music. In this he did not follow the Italian example. Instead of adopting their even, flowing phrases, so well suited to melody, he broke them whenever the action became passionate. His ideal of those days was very Mozartian and had nothing academic or pompous about it; he wished to create an ensemble of beauty, movement, and life. This is why he was bored by the insipid Italian grand opera, so cold, so restricted, so grandiloquent. Soon after his arrival in Rome he wrote: "I am too old for everything except for what is true" (*"Auch da hab' ich wieder gefühlt, dass ich für Alles zu alt bin, nur für's Wahre nicht"*).

Hence his enjoyment of farcical opera, the vivid and unsullied outpouring of the Italian nature. His dream was to bring Moses' staff with him to Germany, the staff which would bring forth water from the rock. Mozart could do it. . . . But Mozart was unique and was soon to die. Ah, why did Goethe wait so long? Why did he not go to him at once? Why did he persist, for fifteen long years, in clinging to his Kayser and trying to shape him according to his will? Kayser was no doubt a worthy man, very dignified, highly moral, religious to the point of renunciation,[186] a good, well-trained musician, but desperately slow—a shadow which vanished into nothing in the light of Goethe, the sun.[187]

In 1789, Kayser definitely retired into his solitude at Zürich, where he remained till his death in 1823. Goethe was faithful to his memory, and never forgot the sorrow which Kayser's abdication caused him.

But this disastrous experience, although it lasted fifteen years, did not discourage him. No sooner did a

G. M. Kraus del:

C. Müller sc.

new collaborator appear than Goethe at once resumed his great schemes for musical drama. This time he worked with Friedrich Reichardt of Königsberg, a brilliant and intelligent man, active, brimming with energy, inventiveness, warmth, and life—the very opposite of Kayser. It was not Goethe who had to go after the musician. Reichardt came and came again; he wrote and wrote again; he gave Goethe no peace.

Together with Johann Abraham Schulz, Reichardt had founded in Berlin the splendid *Lieder* school which in the course of thirty years blossomed over the whole of Germany. . . . The principle of the school was that "the composer's music must interpret the poet's words." Word and sound, phrase and melody, must be one. These were indeed Goethe's own views.

Since 1780 Reichardt had been passionately fond of Goethe's poems, which he was always setting to music. Many of his inspirations were delightful; after a century and a half they still preserve their delicate perfume. With a deep understanding of Goethe's artistic ideas he had an accurate touch for his declamatory passages. In the same scene he would alternate, with the happiest results, instrumental passages and declamation, pass on to the sung recitative and then to the aria, of which he varied the rhythm and the expressive character. He begged Goethe to write an operatic *libretto*, and the poet, encouraging him, conceived the idea of a lyric drama, the characters of which would be inspired by Ossianic lore. He intended to incorporate in this work the Norse mythology and the Sagas.

"I have already formed a plan, of which I will tell you when you come again."[188]

I like to imagine the Norns beginning to weave in the Olympian's brain the destiny threads of the *Wanderer* in Wagner's *Ring*. . . .[189]

He resumed at the same time the subject of the Queen's Necklace, and made of it a light opera in three acts—"*Die Mystifizierten.*"

In Venice he met his composer again, and Reichardt did not allow the promise of an opera *libretto* to grow cold. But Goethe's interest had waned. At this time the demon of natural science was beginning to obsess him, and he had no longer any inclination for these things ("*Kein Gemüt zu allem diesem Wesen*"). However, Reichardt kept close to his heels, and so Goethe returned to Fingal and Ossian. But nothing was to come of it. An evil fate pursued both poet and composer.

Reichardt, whose sympathy with the French Revolution had made him impossible at the court of Berlin, lost his position as *Hofkapellmeister*, a post which gave him every opportunity of producing music-drama. And although Goethe had become, in 1791, the *Oberdirek-*

tor of the Weimar theatre, his provincial stage lacked the necessary equipment for such performances.

He could not even perform his ballad operas there, nor had he any hope of having an opera performed on any other German stage. Now Goethe would never write a theatrical work *in abstracto*, without knowing beforehand the theatre, the actors, and the public for whom the work was intended. He therefore abandoned all idea of this work and buried himself in science (*Farbenlehre*, 1792). Besides this, the events of the time demanded imperiously that the "toga should yield to arms." He left for the campaign against France.[190]

On his return, his friendship with Reichardt, the friend of France, the Jacobin, cooled considerably, and under the influence of Schiller became a distressing enmity after the year 1795.[191]

Zelter replaced Reichardt. In 1796 he commenced his work on Goethe's *Lieder.* Their correspondence began in 1799, and from the beginning of their friendship they found that they were in closest sympathy. As early as 1798, Goethe said that Zelter's *Lieder* were a faithful reproduction of his poetic intentions" ("*eine radikale Reproduktion der poetischen Intentionen*").[192] In 1799 he said, in a letter to him, that while it was true that he had inspired melodies in Zelter, it was no less true that Zelter's melodies had inspired him to write more than one *Lied*. "I feel certain that if we were living together I would be in a more lyric mood than I am at present."

Had Goethe then, at the age of fifty, found at last his musical collaborator, of whom he had dreamt so often?

No. He was only to meet new disappointments of which he never spoke; for Goethe never complained to others, and always buried his sorrows within himself. God knows he was not spared many.

There is no doubt that in Zelter he found his most faithful, affectionate, and devoted friend, a friend who, as it were, took root in him, derived from him all the joy of living, and died when Goethe died.[193] No doubt also this musician became the most accurate interpreter of the ideas in Goethe's *Lieder*, so accurate that, as he told Goethe, "there was no need for him to search for new melodies; all he had to do was to find those which were already in the poet's mind unknown to him."[194]

Zelter, however, failed to understand Goethe's most persistent dream, to create, in collaboration with a musician, great epic and dramatic works. It is possible that Zelter, realizing that he was incapable of carrying these schemes into effect, merely pretended incomprehension. It was a perpetual misunderstanding. In 1799 Goethe sent Zelter his *First Walpurgis Night*, and outlined to him his scheme of composing great dramatic ballads. Zelter, instead of taking advantage of the occasion, asked Goethe to write him an opera *libretto.* Some time before Goethe had thought of writing a Greek tragedy with choruses, *The Danaides*; but he abandoned all idea of it. Zelter's dramatic collaboration was limited to some incidental music for *Egmont* and *Götz von Berlichingen*, at Weimar. Some years later Zelter again asked for a text for an opera, and suggested as a subject, "Hercules" or "Orpheus." The idea of setting to music the first *Faust*, published in 1808, never occurred to him, this task being left to Prince Radziwill.[195] In vain did Goethe ask him to compose at least the music for some of the songs, for instance, the magnificent chorus of spirits, *"Schwindet ihr Dunkeln"* ("Vanish, dark spirits"), when some scenes from *Faust* were performed at Weimar at the end of 1810. Zelter found some excuse for avoiding the task. Thus the unfortunate Goethe was compelled to have recourse to his willing musical factotum, Eberwein, the conductor of his little private choir, who as a composer was below mediocrity. Goethe at first tried him in his monodrama *Proserpina*, and in 1814 he discussed

Faust with him. He went to the trouble of doing all the preparatory work: he shortened the first monologues, shortened the scene with Wagner, changed the whole beginning up to the end of the Easter chorus, "*Euch ist der Meister nah, Euch ist er da*" ("The Master is near you, he is here"), into a single scene in monologue, interrupted only by the apparition of the Spirit of the Earth (*Erdgeist*), and the choruses. He decided that Faust's words should have a soft musical accompaniment, that the approach and the apparition of the Spirit of the Earth were to be treated melodramatically, and that the Easter chorus should be melodious. Eberwein could not understand how music could be introduced into the piece. Goethe made patient efforts to explain the poem to him, induced him to feel the very pulse of the music, tried to make him realize the atmosphere of mystery which pervades Faust's magic laboratory when he opens the book of Nostradamus. . . . Eberwein could not grasp it . . .[196] and Goethe gave it up . . . (spring, 1815).

Next year he formed the great project of which we have already spoken, the oratorio which would stand side by side with the *Messiah*;[197] Zelter was to write the music, and it was to be given at the jubilee of the Reformation. But the realization of such a work soon proved to be hopeless. Zelter was utterly unable to cope with it . . . and Goethe gave it up. . . . (1816).[198]

How many times had Goethe to renounce his hopes! And there, close at hand, was Beethoven, who would have been only too glad to work with him and for him, to set *Faust* to music,[199] and to write, at his dictation, an oratorio after the great example of Handel!

The last blow came in February, 1816, when he wished to present at his theatre a play specially written to celebrate the German victory, *Des Epimenides Erwachen* ("The Awakening of Epimenides"); and the musicians, *his* musicians, scoffed at the work and at him! They had not even the decency to hide it from him. Goethe was deeply hurt. He declared that from that day on he would never permit in Weimar the performance of any new music written for his poems. It was the end of forty years' laborious efforts to wed his poetry to music on the stage. It was a complete and humiliating defeat.[200]

But if the theatre was denied him, if, tired and disappointed, he refused to visit it except on rare occasions, Goethe had still not given up his cherished dream; far from it, for he concentrated on it within himself, on the stage of his own thoughts. He created his own theatre, in perfect freedom, his own invisible opera, his great lyric drama. He gave us the second *Faust.*

There is no doubt of this; we are not putting forward a hypothesis; they are his own words.

It was into this stream of thought that Goethe, throughout his life, directed the torrents of poetry and music which flooded his subconscious being. His aim was that stage representation should include every musical resource—instrumental music, solo voices, choruses as well as scenery. Speaking to Eckermann,[201] Goethe stated, forcibly:

"The first part of *Faust* can only be entrusted to the greatest tragedians. Then, in the operatic part (*im Teile der Oper*), the different characters must be in the hands of the finest singers. The rôle of Helen cannot be played by one artist; two great artists are required for this, for it is very rare that a singer is at the same time a tragedian of the first rank."

But where could a composer be found who combined, in accordance with Goethe's express wish, "the German natural characteristics with the Italian style" (*"welcher seine deutsche Natur mit der italienischen Art und Weise verbände"*)? A second Mozart? . . . Goethe did not appear to be very anxious to find him. It looks as if his ambition to see the actual realization of this great work had diminished almost to vanishing-point. When Eckermann showed signs of impatience, he answered, calmly:

"Let us wait[202] and see what the gods will send us in due time. Such things must not be hurried. The time will come when the significance of this work will become manifest to mankind, and when directors of theatres, poets, and composers will take advantage of it."

He showed no interest in the result. He no longer desired to see the great work on the stage. In his mind he had already seen it.[203]

Thus ended a life's effort to create a new type of theatre. Renunciation and introspection were all that remained.

But the second *Faust* gained by this very fact a far greater value; it was the outcome and the combination of all the dreams of poetry and music which Goethe had accumulated on the stage of his inmost self. How full of light becomes this immense work, which baffled all the critics of the time and broke with all traditional forms! . . . It is a universe in the first stages of creation, when the Spirit moves upon the face of the waters, awaiting the "Let there be light,"—the light of the second Goethe, the musician.[204]

I do not wish, however, in writing thus, to convey the

impression that the second *Faust* is, in my opinion, merely a gigantic *libretto.* A *libretto* is only half a poem. A work by Goethe, even when written for music, is in itself more than a poem. It already contains its music. As Goethe said in the lines which I quoted at the beginning of this essay, *"Nur nicht lesen, immer singen!"* ("Never read, always sing"). The poem is, in itself, a song, but it is much more besides: it is an orchestra. In *Faust*, Parts I and II, Goethe's work is such that it suggests fairy stories of the romantic period in their instrumental setting. It is Wagnerian, and even surpasses the Wagnerian idea.

Philip Spitta has described it well. Goethe, whose aging senses could not respond to the new music, such as Beethoven, Schubert, and Weber, was nevertheless the creator of the poetical world which they illuminated and painted in music. Poetically, he created a music which was even greater than theirs. No musical genius ever did, or ever will express in a *Lied* certain *Lieder* by Goethe, which in two lines express the infinite.

"Ueber allen Gipfeln
Ist Ruh . . ."

"Was . . .
durch das Labyrinth der Brust
Wandelt in der Nacht . . ."

W. Göthe.

nach der Natur gezeichn. am Tage seiner Beerdigung 1832.

"They are too musical to be set to music," said Spitta, profoundly. Only in instrumental music could the expression of such thought be attempted. But even then it would be merely the creation of an atmosphere, a circumambience magical, but, alas, empty. The mighty waves of light which rise and fall on the ocean of sound will always lack the single utterance which should capture them, making them one with the spirit.

Goethe created a *Sprachmusik* (music of speech) and he was its master. When he reigned over his little company of actors in Weimar he made them go through a very strict course of "musical speech." This was particularly the case at the beginning of the century, from 1800 to 1807, and it could almost be said that during that time his company was under Goethe's conductor's bâton. This is not a metaphor, for when conducting the rehearsals of plays he actually used a bâton to indicate rhythm and speed of speech. Like Schiller, Goethe was in arms against the "realist" school and held that tragedy should be modelled on opera. He conceived his company of actors as an orchestra, in which every player subordinates himself to the ensemble and plays his part punctiliously.

He made *Wilhelm Meister* express his ideas on this subject in his speech to the comedians.[205] "In a symphony no player would think of accompanying loudly another player's solo; each endeavours to play in accordance with the spirit and intentions of the composer, and to give a perfect rendering of the part entrusted to him, whether it be important or not. Should we not work with the same precision, with the same intelligence, we who cultivate an art far more elusive than any form of music, for the reason that we have to portray, with taste and understanding, not only the commonest but also the rarest features in human life?"

Wilhelm, thanks to his duke's favour, was to his great delight, master of Philine and the theatrical company.* But his delight did not last long, for Philine became the duke's mistress and the comedians covered him with ridicule. Nevertheless, he carried out his ideas. He conducted the actors as a *Kapellmeister* conducts his singers and his orchestra.[206] He insisted upon strict adherence to his tempi, and his light and shade: *forte, piano, crescendo, diminuendo.* In 1803 Goethe put his ideas into definite form, in his *Rules for Actors* (*Regeln für Schauspieler*). In these he described declamation as a "prose-music"[207] (*"eine prosaische Tonkunst"*). In the producer's copy of his *Bride of Messina* he annotated the text, like a musical score:

* Translator's Note.—Wilhelm Meister is really Goethe himself.

— Here, whispering softly (*halblaut rauschend*).
— Here, clearer with more sound (*heller, klingender*).
— Here, dully (*dumpf*).
— Here, deep and awestruck (*tief, schauerlich*).
— Here, in a different tempo, much quicker (*muss ein anderes, viel schnelleres Tempo gewählt werden*).

These indications, however, did not satisfy him. He wanted one of Maelzel's metronomes, such as Beethoven and the musicians of his time had. For his "music-speech" school he compiled a whole table of "bars" in which the time-length of each word and each pause was given. He even drew a diagram, giving in millimeters, the duration for each punctuation sign.

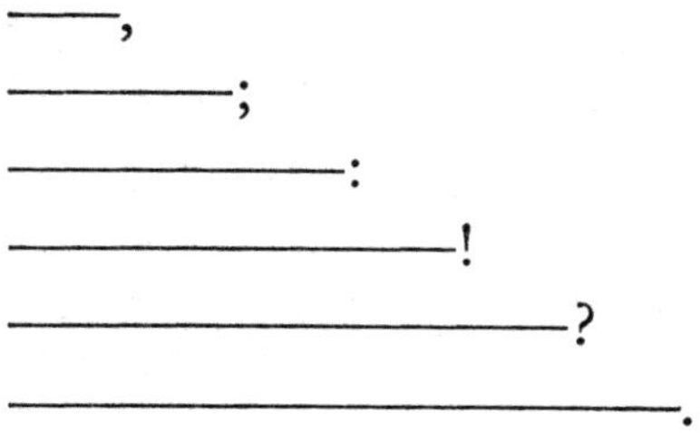

———,
—————;
————————:
——————————!
——————————————?
————————————————.

This fondness for rules and for typically German discipline, threatened at times to kill his creative impulse. The poet cannot hide the drill sergeant! We might suppose that such a method would lead to the mechanical movements of a regiment drilled at a word of command.[208] But Anton Genast tells us that the great instructor used these methods only with beginners and gradually gave them a free hand, as they became masters of their technique.[209]

His actors, however, were not alone in being compelled to submit to the methods of the conductor of an orchestra. Goethe, the master-poet, himself submitted in his creations to the spirit of music. When his poetical genius had reached full maturity (1796-1806) he sometimes wrote down, before beginning the actual composition of the poem, in words which had neither sequence nor sense, the sound effects and the rhythm of the lines. When rhymesters would reproach him for disregarding the traditional rules of metre and rhyme, he would reply:

"Let me enjoy the music of it" (*"Lass mich des-Gesanges geniessen"*).

But this music was not music as conceived by musicians. It was Goethe's ambition to create a new order of music, his own personal achievement,[210] and to establish a form which he considered superior to music without words. When he had drunk his fill of ordinary music the poet-king would raise the sceptre, which he had never for a moment laid aside.

"The beauty of perfected human speech (*Rede*)," he told Knebel, "is far greater than that of song. There is nothing we can compare to it: its inflections and modulations (*Abwechslungen und Mannigfaltig-*

30

31

keiten) in the expression of our feelings (*Gemüt*) are infinite in number.[211] Song must return to simple speech, when the greatest dramatic and emotional heights are to be attained. All the great composers have noticed this."

Music was never to him what it is to great musicians, namely the means of perfecting speech. It is the poet's words which perfect music.

In this both musician and poet are right, if in each case the result is a work of genius, for it absorbs the whole of the world within them, the total ego. The proportions of the elements employed by the ego for its conception and self-expression may vary, but the sum total remains the same. A Goethe is a musician in poetry, just as a Beethoven is a poet in music.[212] Those who are only musicians, those who are only poets, are but minor princes, whose powers do not extend beyond the borders of their little provinces. But Goethe and Beethoven are emperors of the soul of the whole universe.

BETTINA

SILHOUETTE OF GOETHE BEFORE THE BUST OF A DEAD FRIEND (ABOUT 1780)

BETTINA

DURING the short time which has elapsed since the publication, as a serial, of my first studies on *Goethe and Beethoven*, the biography of Bettina has been enriched by new documents, which shed further light on her interesting and many-sided personality. The principal source has at last been tapped. The private archives of Wiepersdorf, the family home of the Arnims, where Bettina's letters had been collected, were jealously guarded by her second son, Siegmund, a companion of Bismarck in his young days and an ultra-conservative, who would not allow any outsider to see his treasure; they were opened, after his death, to a privileged few who were allowed to make a careful scrutiny of Bettina's correspondence with Goethe.[213] But a vast number of letters, sketches and drafts remained untouched.

In 1929 the whole collection was sold. Public opinion in Germany, roused by this dispersal of historic documents, induced private munificence to provide the means of buying up almost immediately and classifying the nucleus of this correspondence, namely all that refers to Goethe; nevertheless many manuscripts were scattered to the four winds. We have been able to discover from the catalogues of antiquaries some of the secrets of the "Goethe-Bettina" enigma. The curtain has been lifted, in part at least, especially on those days in Teplitz, in August, 1810, of which I have written in my first essay, and which must have left on Bettina's mind a far deeper impression than it was wise for Goethe to arouse.

Before quoting here a very intimate letter, over which, as it seems to me, the piety of Goethe's admirers has drawn a veil—a veil which has scarcely been raised—I must recall in a few words to the reader, who may not be so well instructed in this true romance as are the Germans, the principal stages in Bettina's passion for Goethe.

It is indeed a strange and mysterious story, a life's dream, from which the heroine could never free herself, even for a moment. It is a case of invincible autosuggestion, a destiny ordained, as it were, at birth, and, as Bettina would have told us, a reincarnation of love beyond the grave.

Her mother, Maximiliana La Roche, a beautiful woman, native of the Rhine Provinces, was loved by Goethe when he was twenty-three and she was sixteen (1772-73). This love was not a passing infatuation, but Maximiliana, obedient to her parents' wish, married a merchant named Brentano and settled in Frankfurt, where Bettina was born on April 4, 1785.[214]

After her mother's premature death in 1793, Bettina was brought up in a convent, where the works of poets were not accessible to her. So she was seventeen before she read Goethe's poems, which at first she did not understand.[215] During the years which followed, however, she came by degrees to appreciate their charm, and her disposition, which was wholesome, fresh, and spontaneous, set her apart from the malevolent prudishness of Cassel society, the people who expressed disgust at *Egmont's* "vulgarities" and at the poet's "platitudes." This innocent attraction for Goethe had, however, no personal character, until that fateful day in June, 1806, when, at her father's house in Offenbach, she discovered by chance eighty-four letters from Goethe to her grandmother, Sophie La Roche, written between 1772 and 1775, full of the young man's adoration of her mother.

This revelation had an overwhelming effect on the young girl. She copied the whole correspondence several times. (One of these copies was sold by auction last year.) She learnt them by heart. And this sensitive dreamer, to whose burning eyes the beauties of nature were an open book, bore henceforth upon her heart the impress of Goethe's young love. This may justly be termed, speaking scientifically, a phenomenon of obsession, which nothing could efface; it was beautiful, it was touching, but it had its dangerous side.

On October 21, 1809, she wrote to Goethe, in a state of melancholy ecstasy:

"I really believe that I have inherited this feeling from my mother. She must have known (*erkannt*) you intimately. She must have possessed (*genossen*) you fully when I was coming into the world. . . ."

What was her thought? That she was Goethe's daughter (*"das Kind"*)?[216] Perhaps. But she certainly imagined that she was the child of his *love*, and that this love returning from beyond the grave to Goethe the beloved, to Goethe the lover—had taken upon itself her bodily presence.

This love-stricken folly found forthwith the environment in which it could best thrive. In the same month in which she discovered the correspondence she hastened to Goethe's mother, Aja, who, when she spoke of her "little boy," was as exaggeratedly sensitive as Bettina. She declared that she was cruelly separated from him by the distance from Frankfurt to Weimar—actually only a few hours—but to her an eternity. . . . The two love-stricken women, the old and the young, both full of fantastic ideas, both warm-hearted, found in the love of their common idol the path to each other's affection.

The old woman poured into the girl's ear a never-ending stream of gossip, her triumphant recollections of the child Goethe, which Bettina drank in like parched soil under a shower. We can imagine how, in such circumstances, the obsession took root and flourished.

In the following spring she paid her first visit to Goethe (April 23, 1807). . . . In those days travel was no easy matter; war was raging throughout the country. In order to accompany her brother-in-law, Jordis, from Cassel to Berlin, whence they proceeded later to Weimar, she and her sister had donned men's clothes. It reminds us of a scene from *As You Like It.* Finally Bettina arrived alone, her heart beating violently, almost fainting with emotion, at Goethe's door. She had a letter of introduction from Wieland, who presented her as the daughter and granddaughter of beloved friends who were no more.

Shall I describe this well-known meeting once again? It has been told so well by Fritz Bergmann, who, after a careful scrutiny of the somewhat embellished account of the incident which Bettina gave later, has verified the essential points, and has with delicacy expressed her emotion. Both the old man and the young woman shared it. For him, what a flood of remembrances: it was indeed the beloved dead who came to see him. . . . For her, what a mingled torrent of joy and fear: she stood tongue-tied, at one moment overcome, at another peacefully content. There followed a strange reaction, at which some have foolishly sneered, though it was the most natural in the world; exhausted with emotion, the young girl lost consciousness and fell asleep on Goethe's knees, in his arms.[217] The fainting fit lasted but a few moments. Goethe was very kind to her. He was deeply touched by the elemental force of emotion in his "little Mignon." He spoke to her affectionately, and at length, dismissing impatiently the inquisitive Christiana who had opened the door and asked him to go out with her. With the sweet messenger from the past, he reviewed the days of his boyhood, felt his youth reawaken in the cramped atmosphere of Weimar, and with a symbolic gesture, full of significance for the young dreamer who doubtless saw in it a token of mystic betrothal, he placed a ring upon her finger.[218]

Later Goethe appreciated the danger. When the young enthusiast poured out in a letter to Goethe's mother the longings of her heart—the mother did her best to fan the flame—[219] and when the old lady had sent him an account of the ardent feeling which he had aroused in Bettina, Goethe knitted his brows and withdrew in stubborn silence. To Bettina's first letters there was no single word of reply.

So Bettina went to seek the answer which she could not otherwise obtain. She returned to Weimar, at the beginning of November, 1807, this time accompanied by a throng of relatives—Clemens, Arnim, her sister Gunda, and her brother-in-law Savigny. She stayed in Weimar for ten days, seeing Goethe almost every day, and Goethe began to enjoy her company. Bettina noticed this and showed herself at her best; with her naïve and spring-like charm she elicited friendly smiles; she was original and alluring and gave free rein to the impulses of her spontaneous fancy. During these familiar talks, these walks on Goethe's arm, their intimacy had made such progress that when she wrote to him again, some weeks later, she used the familiar "thou," and henceforth continued to do so.[220]

Goethe, however, was still on the defensive; another

year passed before he, too, wrote "thou."[221] But his "you" was only a weak defence, and Bettina knew it. When, on November 10th, they parted, Goethe kissed her,[222] and soon did more for her than use the intimate "thou" in his letters. When she wrote him letters, aflame with love, he sent her back her own words like jewels in the magnificent setting of two sonnets. It was as if he entered into Bettina's deepest self, till both merged into one. We know what artists are, how mighty a force for deception lies in their impressionable nature; it is their peculiar failing, and we are not the dupes of their florid declarations. But how different must have been the impression upon Bettina. . . . In February, 1808, she told Goethe that never before had she looked upon a man,[223] and that it hurt her to think that all her youth was being wasted. . . . "But now I have you. . . ."

She was intelligent enough not to confine her letters to love; she dealt with poetry also; she wrote of *Egmont*, which she appreciated and discussed in striking fashion, and a little later of *"Wahlverwandtschaften"* ("Elective affinities").

Her delight in Goethe's art was like the primitive delight of a child bathing in the sea. She discussed music with him and showed a virile taste for Cherubini's *Medea* and for Gluck's *Iphigenie auf Tauris*;

following the wise promptings of heart and mind, she constituted herself the provider of music for Goethe's private choir; she sent him curious documents and succeeded more than any other woman of his circle in appealing to his intellect.[224]

After the death of Goethe's mother, Aja (September 13, 1808), the poet's letters to Bettina show a far more affectionate tone. Now that his mother had gone, Bettina was the only one who knew the essential details of his younger days which Goethe himself had forgotten. She was the sole keeper of all those precious memories which she had gathered from the lips of his own mother. He wrote to her a year later:[225] "Your letters give me great pleasure: they remind me of the time when I was perhaps as foolish as you but certainly happier and better than today."

His smile could scarcely hide a feeling of regret and of melancholy. The months which followed showed that his affection increased. Goethe could resist no longer.[226] So much so, that when Bettina interrupted her correspondence for a few weeks, Goethe felt her silence very keenly, and wrote to her on May 10, 1810: "Dear Bettina, I have not heard from you for a very long time;[227] I cannot leave for Karlsbad without sending you greetings, without calling upon you—by letter —and without receiving from you a sign of life. Your letters accompany me. When I am there, they must replace your charming presence. . . ." (We feel that Goethe is here restraining his feelings.) "I can say no more, for in truth there is nothing I can give you; it is either you who give everything or you who take everything. . . ."

During the following summer months Bettina met Beethoven, and brimming over with the impression which he had made upon her, went to see Goethe in Teplitz and remained with him for three days, from August 9 to 12, 1810.

What happened during those three days? The unusual warmth of Goethe's letter, written to Bettina immediately after her visit, suggests that she had never been more favoured by her idol. I have shown this in my first essay, but there were many gaps in my story. Bettina's long letter of July 6-28, 1810, stopped suddenly in the middle of a sentence in which she spoke of Beethoven. From July 28th to October 18th there was a lull in the correspondence which is all the more difficult to understand, as Goethe in his short letter, written on August 17th, five days after Bettina's departure from Teplitz, spoke with unusual enthusiasm of the many pages (*Blätter*)[228] which Bettina had left him, and which he "read over and over again"; he spoke also of one which had just arrived. . . . What did he do with them, what did they contain, these letters which Bettina did not find in the collection which Councillor von Müller sent her after Goethe's death, in August, 1832? What is perhaps even more extraordinary is that Bettina, the last person to disguise her feelings—she would much rather have exaggerated them—did not rewrite them. She never wished to disturb the dust of those recollections.

Here, however, are a few grains from the heap, discovered last year, among the drafts of Bettina's letters which were sold under the hammer and which have not been mentioned in any of the books on her:

"The twilight of evening was falling, this hot August day. . . . He was sitting at the open window, while I stood before him, my arms round his neck, my eyes piercing his to their depths, like an arrow. Perhaps he could withstand my gaze no longer, for, to break the silence, he asked me whether I felt hot and whether I would not like to be cooler? . . . I nodded assent. He went on, 'Why not open your breast (*Mach doch den Busen frei*) to the evening breeze?' As I did not object, although I blushed, he undid my bodice, looked at me, and said: 'The glow of the sunset has reddened (*eingebrannt*) your cheeks.' He kissed my breast and rested his head on it. 'No wonder,' said I, 'for my sun is sinking to rest upon my bosom.' He gazed at me for a long time and we were both silent. He then asked, 'Has anyone ever touched your breast?' 'No,' I replied; 'it is so strange that you should touch me thus.' Then he showered kisses on me, many, many, violent kisses. . . . I was frightened. . . . He should have let me go; and yet it was so strangely beautiful. In spite of myself I smiled, yet feared that this happiness should not last. His burning lips, his stifled breath—it was like lightning. I was in a whirl of confusion; my curly hair hung in loose strands. . . . Then he said, softly: 'You are like a storm; your hair falls like rain, your lips dart lightning, your eyes thunder.' 'And you, like Zeus, knit your brows and Olympus trembles.' 'When you undress at night, in the future, and the stars shine as now upon your breasts, will you remember my kisses?' 'Yes.' 'And will you remember that I should like to cover your bosom with as many kisses as there are stars in heaven?' . . . The memory of it tears me asunder (*zerreist mich von allen Seiten*), I long to dissolve in tears like a cloudy sky.—Never repeat what I confide to you this lonely night. I have never told it to anyone before. . . !"[229]

These ashes which we have just stirred still burn! What a glow do their embers throw on a letter which Goethe wrote some days later. What a light is shed on those written during the winter 1810-11, which still exist, apart from the letters from Bettina which were destroyed and to which Goethe refers.

"Bettina, dearest of all! (*allerliebste*) Your letters are such that the latest seems always the most fascinating! Thus it was with the pages which you brought me, and which I read hungrily, again and again, on the morning you left me. But now comes your last letter which surpasses (*übertrifft*) all the others. If you can go on surpassing yourself (*überbieten*), do it! With yourself you have taken away so much, that it is only fair that you should send me back something. . . ."

To this letter he pinned a note asking her to send her reply not to Teplitz, nor to Weimar, but to Dresden, in care of a third person, and he added, "Oh dear, what will your letter tell me? . . ."

We, too, should like to know. What did this letter contain, and those which followed, for more than one was written before October. During that month the correspondence which was saved from destruction began again with a letter from Goethe, who had returned to Weimar on October 25th, in which he says that he should have thanked Bettina long ago "for the dear letters which reached me in due course (*nach und nach*), and particularly for remembering the 27th of August so kindly. . . ." It is lost to us, like all the rest, this souvenir of August 27th. All we know is that

Goethe did not reply to the letters after his note of August 17th. He had set a gulf between this memory and himself. And now, instead of reverting to the past, we see the path into which he would direct Bettina's ardent sensibility; he took advantage of her frame of mind—he well knew how to handle loving hearts—to ask her to tell him all the interesting secrets which his mother, Aja, had confided to her, all those stories of his youth which he remembered no longer. He was rather troubled about them; who knows what Juliet's nurse told Romeo of her nursling? . . . It was a great sacrifice which he asked of Bettina, for these stories were her personal treasure, to which no one else had access. How deeply Bettina must have loved him to do what he asked; we feel what it must have meant to her. Goethe, however, could not have chosen a more favourable moment to secure this sacrifice from her.[230]

She complied with his wish. But she was not altogether unaware of his motive, as is shown by her reply of November 4th:

"You have always some good reason for writing to me. But my heart retains nothing of your letter except the last words, 'love me until we meet again' (*Liebe mich bis zum Wiedersehen*!) If you had not added these last words, I should perhaps have taken more careful note of the motive prompting the request which preceded them; but this single proof of affection has defeated me. . . . A thousand tender thoughts have held me captive last night, and all today. And now I realize that what you demand (*verlangst*) is so precious to me that I find it worthy of your acceptance."

Thereupon she threw open the sanctuary of her recollections. Is it not as if, in giving them to him, she gave herself again? She expresses a great deal in the following words, which sound so profoundly sincere: "*Ich bin ein duftender Garten dieser Erinnerungen*" ("I am a fragrant garden wherein these reflections flower").

She threw them to him by the armful, these flowers of the past, which he planted afresh in his *Dichtung und Wahrheit.*

From this moment, however, I find a new tone in Bettina's letters. There is disturbance, sorrow, a passion imperious and burdensome; there are spiteful fits in which she inveighs against Goethe's friends and particularly against his "house god," Zelter. There are, indeed, many heavy clouds in her sky.

"Since we were together in Teplitz I find it impossible to pay you compliments."[231]

". . . Once I climbed a mountain top. . . . What is it that weighs so heavily on my heart? . . ."

Goethe remained impervious to the allusions in these letters, their cries of passion, their attacks on Zelter; he was deaf to the passionate dreamer with her strange soliloquies on music, thoughts like lightning flashes in the darkness of the night. . . . He took good care not to upset her. He did not waste his time: he gathered all these priceless recollections which she had inherited from his mother. It was Bettina who gave, gave without end. . . .

But was he, too, not giving, giving in even a larger measure than she? He was her love! He was her life! Was it not she who wrote: "If you only knew how often a single word of yours delivers me from the horrors of a crushing dream. Oh, tell me: 'Yes, child, I am within you'! Then all is well—— Tell me! ——."[232]

When Goethe needed Bettina no longer he grew tired of her. No doubt he would. It is no easy matter to feel that one is so indispensable to another! Did not Bettina's hungry heart ask that Goethe should be "within her," should belong to her?[233] Such a man as Goethe could belong only to those who assumed no proprietary rights over his freedom. That is why he preferred his fat, amiable Christiana to Bettina with the exigencies of her love.

Besides this, there was a deep misunderstanding

Bettine

between them. The Goethe whom Bettina loved was not the Goethe of her time. The one she loved was the Goethe of her mother, of the days of the first *Wilhelm Meister*. . . . Where are the snows—where is the fire —of yesteryear?

Eckermann, asked by Moritz Carrière what Goethe's relations were with Bettina, replied: "She always loved him, but she was often a nuisance; she asked the old man to undertake what he had done long ago, as a young man. She would tell him: 'Art and antiquity, what's that? (*Was Kunst und Altertum?*) You must write a *Götz von Berlichingen*; that's better!' And he would reply: 'I have written it. To each thing its proper time.' "[234]

I shall not refer again to the fatal rupture, which Goethe had determined upon and which took place between him and Bettina in 1811, in spite of her efforts to renew her relations with him. Christiana provided the occasion, but even without Christiana the break would have occurred. In vain did Bettina write to Goethe again in 1817. He did not answer, and her attempts to enter his house by surprise only irritated him the more.

Finally, however, he could not but be moved by the unwavering loyalty of the friend whom he had rebuffed. It was particularly her scheme for a monument to him in Frankfurt[235] which softened his heart and showed his human weakness. He decided that he would let her know how much he was touched. . . .

It was a supreme consolation decreed by fate! Twelve days before his death, on March 10, 1832, a young messenger from Bettina came to see him, Siegmund von Arnim, her second son, who was then eighteen. The mother's letter said, "Embrace me anew in this child" (*"Umfasse mich neu in diesem Kinde"*). Goethe was kind and fatherly. He invited him to his table and saw him daily, until he was stricken by the illness from which he never recovered. Mignon's son was his last visitor, and the lines which he wrote in Siegmund's album were Goethe's farewell to the world.[236] When the young man left him, Goethe was already ailing, and on his arrival in Frankfurt he heard of his death. We still have the letter which he wrote from there to his mother. Bettina was anxious to know if Goethe remembered her, and what he had said. His son could only tell her that Goethe had praised her talent:

"It will seem little to you, very little, but not to me. If you had seen him, already lost to this world,[237] but turning the pages of life as in a book, you would have thanked him from your heart for his friendly enquiries about all that concerns you. . . ."

Bettina learnt of his death from a short paragraph in a newspaper which she found on the table, late at night when she came back from a reception. There the news was already known, but no one dared to tell her. We can imagine what that night must have been. But we should be wrong in assuming that this strong-willed woman, far stronger than we are apt to think, was plunged in a romantic grief. The blow which struck her could not touch the Goethe whom she had created for herself—the Goethe whom she had enshrined in her heart.

She could say, rather: "You can no longer escape me! Now I hold you for ever . . ."

Her letter to Councillor von Müller, written at the beginning of April, 1832, is proof of the nobility of her love, which was in truth stronger than death:

"Goethe's death has indeed made upon me an impression deep and ineffaceable, but in no way sorrowful. If words fail me to express the actual truth of what I feel I can describe the glorious impression to you by a picture. He is risen from the dead, he is transfigured, he beholds from Heaven his friends whose souls, to their last breath, are fed by him. . . . I am one of those who have no life except in him! I do not speak *of* him, I speak *to* him, and his replies are my fullest consolation. He leaves no question of mine unanswered, no tender word or prayer without response. How could I be other than happy in the thought that at last he has attained that eternal bliss for which his whole earthly life had been a preparation? And now, here lies the path of my duty: I must cling so close to him that nothing may assume a stronger claim than his. By his side everything that life may bring me henceforth shall but strengthen my communion with him. Thus shall all that is worthy of survival in my earthly existence bear testimony to my love and to his blessing."

She kept her word. And if the remainder of her life was not free from weaknesses—and why should it have been? She was essentially a woman, and that is why we love her—it remained under the ægis of the two gods to whom from the cradle her life had been dedicated, Love and Dreams, "*Traum und Liebe.*" . . . These words would be a fitting title to her famous correspondence published in 1835, *Goethes Briefwechsel mit einem Kinde*, in which, revising her original letters, she pours forth the flood of that inner consciousness which memory had released. Can we blame her? History, which since then has inquired into what she said, has sifted the dream from the reality.[238] But history must, in the end, testify to the loyalty of her heart. And if a heart so loving has led her sometimes to embroider dreams on the background of her story, she has never knowingly altered the design. Her love and her person were always allied with legend and whatever she touched became legendary. Yet she was real. And if, sometimes, her opinion of others deceived her, she has never deceived others, or herself, about her own nature.

This inner life of Bettina has by no means received the attention which it deserves. Enquiry has been focussed almost exclusively on her relations with Goethe. But no matter how intense this love may have been, we must not think that Bettina had no existence outside it. It is true that her whole outlook was illuminated by the burning flame of remembrance; but its boundaries extend far beyond Goethe's life and even beyond his thoughts.

The abundant harvest of Bettina's literary activity has been studied in part. Without referring to it further here, there is much to be said of her ideas in music,[239] of her voluminous correspondence with the famous men of her day, Alexander von Humboldt, Jacob and Wilhelm Grimm, Schleiermacher, Emmanuel Arago, Moritz Carrière, Peter Cornelius, Emmanuel Geibel, Friedrich Christoph Foerster, and others. Lastly there is her political activity.

Fortunate circumstances and the authority which she had gained secured her direct access to those in highest authority, the princes[240] and the king of Prussia, and her courage did not fail her. Neither respect for their exalted position nor fear of displeasing them restrained her. She spoke openly and forcibly. She had decided for herself upon the ideal of what a prince should be—the servant of the community—and this ideal she meant to impress upon them. "Everything belongs to the people," she wrote to the *Kronprinz* of Würtemberg. "Let the prince go lacking, but the people must be free from want." The princes were both flattered and intimidated by the onslaught of this Deborah, the anointed of Goethe. They dared not protest too much. The year 1848 was coming, and its spirit was already weakening the sovereign power. This power was to return, with a vengeance, later on.

Bettina had a splendid colleague in Berlin, Alexander von Humboldt, the last survivor, with her, of Goethe's great brotherhood. He helped her with all his energy and defended her books against the censor,[241] for whom both had a feeling of utter contempt and hatred;[242] he supported her projects and brought her letters to the notice of the king, who was spared the

33

criticism of neither of them. Acting together, they were a real power, and King Frederick William IV had reason to fear their opinions. Certain interesting and unpublished documents which have been communicated to me by a granddaughter of Bettina, Madame Irène Forbes-Mosse, describe Bettina as a Portia pleading unceasingly the cause of the victims of the social order. "At a time when there was no *Landtag* (state Parliament) in Prussia, nor freedom of the press to ventilate wrongs, it was Bettina who brought them all before the king."

Among the bundles of documents relating to such cases, which passed under the hammer last year, I notice first the case of the poet and professor, Hoffmann von Fallersleben, who was disgraced and dismissed from his post on account of his *Unpolitische Lieder.* Then that of the great manufacturer, F. W. Schlöffel, the spokesman of the miserable Silesian weavers, who had been imprisoned on a charge of communism and high treason.[243] Bettina took up his cause and collected personally the material for an *Armenbuch* (Book of the Poor). In 1846 she appears as the champion of the Polish revolutionary Mieroslawski, who had been imprisoned and condemned to death; he was pardoned, thanks to her vehement intervention.[244] In 1849 it was the case of the revolutionary

Kinkel, who was under death sentence. Bettina spent days and nights defending him, writing letter after letter to the king, who replied to her with equal insistence. In my collection are some drafts of unpublished letters by Bettina which are written in her most passionate style:

"You say that Kinkel has been prompted by evil motives. This may be, but the stupidity of putting a man to death because he is a charge on society, and the folly of a law which authorizes such a crime, fills me with revolt. . . . What do his faults matter! It is not this particular man who matters. What matters is that it should no longer be possible for one drop of a man's blood to be shed when that man is in the power of the sovereign."

It must be admitted that the king listened to the arguments of the Angel of Revolution with a respect and a patience which are a testimony in favour both of himself and of Bettina. In 1847 he wrote to her, about Mieroslawski:

"You love loyalty and truth and demand it in others; you yourself are an example of both. But loyalty and truth do not cease to be loyalty and truth even when the lips of a king express them."[245]

Bettina, however, became too outspoken in her feverish attempts, and finally wounded the king's pride. A break occurred at the end of 1847. At the same time she was engaged in a struggle with the Municipality of Berlin, was accused of lèse-majesté and sentenced to two months' imprisonment.

"You condemn," she wrote to Pauline Steinhäuser, "my political tendencies. I have never undertaken anything, unless my inner self compelled me to it (*ich habe nie etwas unternommen was nicht ein Muss in mir gewesen wäre*). Nor have my actions proved without benefit to humanity. There are many whose heads are still on their shoulders, who would have lost them if I had not fought desperately."[246]

She gave her support to the risings of 1848, as did another friend of Beethoven and Goethe, Wilhelmine Schroeter-Devrient. In her letters Bettina lashed the treacherous behaviour of the king and praised the people. But calumny and hatred accumulated forces against her. In April, 1848, she wrote to Pauline Steinhäuser:

"Believe me if they could have thrown me into the ditch it would have been done."[247]

She never flinched from her task: she remained indomitable, facing her foes, even after the ruin of her hopes for democracy. She was "*Freiheitsbegeisterte*" ("intoxicated with ideas of freedom") to the end of her days.[248] Such was her prestige, such was the glamour which she owed to Goethe, her master, that after

1848 the King of Prussia and the princes, in spite of their bitter feelings, treated her with the highest consideration and interested themselves, 1851-52, in the realization of her project of a monument to Goethe at Weimar. But the proud Bettina declined the royal offer to carry out the work, saying that "Goethe's monument could only come from the German people (*weil Goethe nur in deutschen Volk ein Denkmal erhalten könne*)."[249]

It was the attitude of one completely aloof. In spite of the king's pressing invitations, she never went to court.[250] Her life became more and more retired; small and frail in her conventual robe of coarse black cloth, she meditated in her room, which she never left except in the evening to hear quartet music in her Pompeian hall—Joachim was first violin. The idols of her youth, Beethoven and Goethe, illuminated the evening of her days. She remained faithful to them, not as the guardian of their graves, but as the ministrant to the immortal flame of their lives. She had two ardent disciples in her eldest daughters, Armgart and Gisela, both artists like their mother; they were painters, especially Gisela, who married Hermann Grimm; they were musicians, Armgart especially, whom Joachim admired; Gisela also wrote for the stage. All three were eager to succour the downtrodden and to welcome the champions of rebellion. Mother and daughters alike bore on their foreheads the trace of the blood which *Berlichingen* and *Egmont* shed for the freedom of the people.

APPENDICES

THE "MARSEILLAISE" IN GERMANY

SILHOUETTE OF GOETHE ON HORSEBACK

THE "MARSEILLAISE" IN GERMANY[251]

THE *Marseillaise* became known throughout Germany almost as soon as in France. It was first sung in September, 1792, five months after the *War Hymn for the Rhine Army* was composed at Strasbourg on the night after the news of the declaration of war (April 25, 1792). This was a few weeks after the revolutionaries of Marseilles had spread it through Paris (about August 10th). It was sung, not during the battle of Valmy, but a few days after, on the order of the Minister for War, as a *Te Deum* of solemn thanksgiving. The heir to the throne of Prussia, who had heard it in the course of the negotiations which resulted in the retirement of the German army, expressed a desire for the music and received one of the copies sent from Paris to Kellermann[252] (Comp. Revue *La Révolution Française* November-December, 1918; an article by

Julien Tiersot commenting upon extracts from the unpublished memoirs of General Beaufort). After Jemmapes, where the *Marseillaise* made its first appearance on the battle-field, Kotzebue apostrophized the author as follows: "Brute, barbarian, how many of my brothers have you not slain?" The saying seems to have been taken up and repeated by Klopstock in another form. According to a German tradition, Klopstock visited Rouget de Lisle in Hamburg in 1797, and expressed his admiration of this war song, the inspiration of armies. "You are a terrible man; you have cut to pieces 50,000 honest Germans" (*Brockhaus Konversations-Lexikon.* 9th and 10th editions, 1853: on the words *Marseillaise* and *Rouget de Lisle.* N. B.—The editions of the *B. K. Lexikon* of the first forty years of the century do not mention the *Marseillaise*).

Goethe mentions it on three occasions in his history of the *Siege of Mainz.* It is remarkable that only once in these three passages does he refer to the *Marseillaise*, which was performed by the French garrison when they left Mainz, as being a striking piece of music. On the other two occasions it was played with *"Ca ira"* by the oboes of the German regiments to enliven Goethe's guests "while they emptied bottles of champagne." At the dinner tables in hotels the guests asked for it to be played, "and all those present seemed pleased and satisfied with it." This shows that the Germans generally looked upon it as a lively air and took no notice of the words.

A curious example of this has been pointed out to me by Professor Max Friedlaender. Ever since 1804, part of the melody of the *Marseillaise* had spread through Germany, becoming acclimatized as a popular song, which was soon a great favourite. It had become nothing more or less than a romantic highwayman's song—*Rinaldo Rinaldini*, in eleven verses.

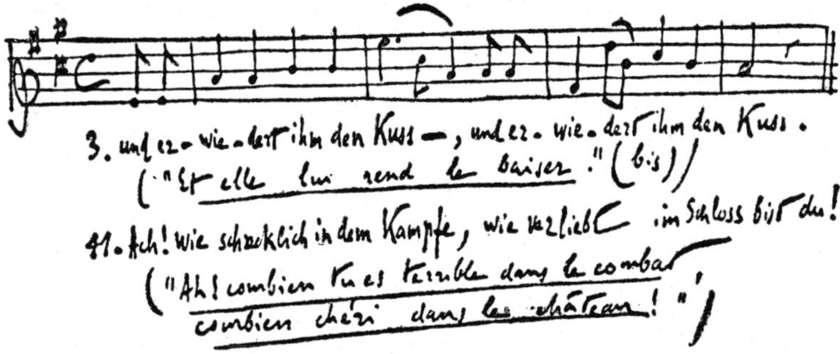

But it was none other than Goethe's brother-in-law, Christian August Vulpius, who had introduced the words of this song into his romance *Rinaldo Rinaldini*, in 1799. In 1804 an unknown composer added the melody which is still sung by the German people of our present day (*Volkslieder von der Mosel und der Saar*. Halle, 1896, No. 336, published by Köhler & Meier). It is, however, very questionable whether

Goethe, or Vulpius himself, recognized the *Marseillaise* in this new form. As we have seen earlier in this book,[253] it was the minor passage in the *Marseillaise* which impressed it on Goethe's mind, while in the popular song of the brave highwayman only the major tune was used.

The fine character of the *Marseillaise* was not really appreciated by German musicians till after 1830.

The Gallic cock under the threefold motto of the Revolution aroused from sleep the national hymn which had been put aside or suppressed under the Empire and the Restoration.[254] It is known that Schumann used the *Marseillaise* three times: in 1839, in the *Viennese Carnival*, in which he concealed it under the guise of a 3-4 time *Ländler*, because the song itself was banned by Metternich; in 1840 in the famous song, Heine's *Two Grenadiers* (the poem was set to music that same year also by Wagner, in Paris, with the same use of the *Marseillaise*); in 1851 in the overture to *Hermann und Dorothea.*

How Beethoven would have been struck by this music, so closely akin to his! The impression would have been far more powerful than in Schumann's case. It would have floated like an ensign above some mighty work of his. Must he not have heard it on his journey from Bonn to Vienna in November, 1792, when he crossed the French lines? Did not the *Marseillaise* reach Austria and force an entry into his deaf ears? The researches of Professor Max Friedlaender among the newspapers and musical publications in Austria, during the first half of the nineteenth century, have revealed nothing. But in any case Beethoven had had relations in Vienna with great musicians who, like Cherubini, had played a large part in the orchestral and choral art of the French Revolution, and it is stated that Salieri, whom Beethoven had known since boyhood and who was a well-known authority in Vienna, used the *Marseillaise* in one of his works called *Palmira*, in 1795. The question may never be answered. But I am inclined to think that had he known it, he would have spoken of it and that one of his compositions would have shown its traces.

APPENDICES

BETTINA'S LETTER ON MUSIC

WEIMAR: TOWER OF THE
CASTLE AND THE DUNGEON

BETTINA'S LETTER ON MUSIC[255]

EMOTION and subconscious impulses, which in all arts and sciences are the source of the supernatural,[256] have, in the case of music, reached the highest point. This is a matter into which no one, as it seems, would wish to probe deeply. We always find, in the background, the mediocrity of the pedants; it is an annihilating force.[257] All of them desire to express themselves by reasoning in music, [and the quintessence of music is that it begins at the precise point where reason ends].[258]

These people, in all good faith and simple-mindedness, believe that expression by reason is possible, and unconsciously employ magic formulas. In some cases only half of these are used; in others the end of the formula is used, before the beginning; so that, instead of being full of life and brilliance, as they were once, the compositions become fixed, frozen, and unutterably tiresome.

Yet, in our hearts a secret stirring is felt; it comes and goes, it disappears again, without betraying its origin. Then, in a moment, genius, hidden for so long in the disorder of chaos, growing and developing, step by step, breaks forth in all its splendour. . . . [Beethoven]. Such is the condition of music today. In this art, genius is always alone, always misunderstood, for it has sought its own path, not, in the full light of day, but almost unconsciously, almost without knowledge of itself.

Many men must be born before a genius appears. And on the other hand, genius must have an active and persistent influence on mankind.[259] Otherwise it would not be genius. Without a public there would be no music.

How keen a delight it is to see, as through a crystal glass, into past centuries, and watch how intelligence governs work, guides its accomplishment, and gives impulse to the spirit of man. . . . In music that will never be again. The flame which now burns no more had its own temple, and that temple is in ruins. Now it is not in our intelligence, but in our hearts,[260] in our own individual temperament, that the spirit of music must be heard. But where is the musician who can keep himself so innocent, so pure that he will only feel, and express—what is Good?

. . . .

How strange is the destiny of the language of music, that it should not be understood! Hence the reason for the furious outcries against everything that has not been heard before—not only because it is not understood, but also because it is not even known. Man,[261] in the presence of music, becomes rigid like a block of wood.[262] What he knows he is prepared to endure, not because he understands it, but because he is used to it, as a donkey is used to its daily load. Never yet have I met anyone who did not turn away from music, weary and depressed, after he had listened to it for a certain time. This is a necessary consequence which it is easier to understand than the contrary. What else can a man do who has vast ambitions,[263] if he does not first rid himself of all these mere artisans of music,[264] if he does not live his own life with which no other man may interfere? . . . He may well "make" music, but he will never set the spirit free from the letter and from the law. Every art claims that it outlives death and leads man to realms that are not of this earth; but there, wherever the Philistines mount guard, man stands in his humiliation with the cropped head of a slave. What should be freedom of will, freedom of life, becomes a mere piece of machinery.[265] We may wait, and believe, and hope—but nothing will happen. We cannot reach the heights save by paths now deeply buried in the sand; our salvation must be by prayer, by the concentration of the heart, and by keeping our faith for ever in our God. Here we face the inaccessible peaks, yet it is only upon their summit that we may inhale with rapture the breath of our desire.[266]

REFERENCES

REFERENCES

[1] It seems most appropriate to put Beethoven's letter "To the Immortal Beloved" into the year 1812 (see my article in Henry Prunière's *Revue Musicale*, October 1, 1927).

[2] "To thank you for the long time I have known you (for I have known you since my childhood's days) is so little for so great a gift . . ." (Beethoven's letter to Goethe, April 12, 1811.)

[3] Conversation with Rochlitz, July, 1822.

[4] In the same year appeared the first part of *Faust*. But Bettina had forestalled him in this plan. Ever since mid January, 1808, she was "submerged" (*versunken*) in *Faust* composition. She wrote Marguerite's moving "Prayer to the Virgin." Beethoven was looking for some one to adapt *Faust* for the theatre (*Cottasches Morgenblatt*, October, 1808). But he can find no one to help him. In 1822, when Rochlitz, who knew nothing of the original project, sends Beethoven the proposal of the Editor Haertel that he should write the music for *Faust*, "Ha!" cries Beethoven, his arms on high. "That would be a task! That should be something worth doing . . ." And he meditates upon it. But at his age, he can do no more; he is engaged on the work of the two great symphonies and of an oratorio. With regret he declines the proposal.

[5] The German phrase is so rich in accumulated energy that in a translation it must be expanded, so that nothing may be lost. "*Ausladen . . . von . . . nach . . . hin . . .*" suggest a torrential discharge, but a discharge directed upon a mark. It is the expression both of the will and of the power of nature.

[6] It is worth noting that Bettina, who quotes these words, is personally of a very different opinion; she says that music adds nothing to Goethe's *Lieder*. Her account, therefore, bears all the more the stamp of authenticity.

[7] Further on in this book will be found a short essay on her psychological life.

[8] This refers to the comparison between the authentic letters, which have been discovered recently, and the edited letters which Bettina published in 1835, after the death of Beethoven and Goethe (*Goethes Briefwechsel mit einem Kinde*). I mention particularly Dr. Waldemar Oehlke's philological thesis *Bettina von Arnim's Briefromane*, 1905, *Bettinas Briefwechsel mit Goethe*, compared with the originals and published in 1922 by Reinhold Steig, and *Bettinas Leben und Briefwechsel mit Goethe*, published by Fritz Bergemann, 1927.

[9] Let us begin by establishing exactly the age and the moral condition of our three heroes at this epoch of 1810. Goethe was sixty-one. He had at last married, in October, 1806, Christiana, with whom he had been living for eighteen years, and whom he had much trouble even then to get the society of Weimar to receive. His son August was seventeen. Four years later (in September, 1814) he was to meet Marianna von Willemer, and a new spring to blossom in his heart, immortalized in the *Westöstlicher Divan.* At the time of which we are speaking he seemed to be enveloped in his distrust of the new spirit of the age and of the younger generation; he was engrossed in the official order of things and in the tenets of respectability. We shall see this only too well in the pages which follow.

Beethoven was forty. He was in the prime of life, flaming with passions. He had just composed the "Appassionata," the "Farewell" Sonata (*Lebewohl*), The Harp Quartet, the E. Flat Concerto, and was writing *Egmont.* Bettina found him smarting from a recent love disappointment; he was still madly in love with Theresa Malfatti. He saw the foolishness of it, flogging himself with the whip of his bitter irony. Bettina's advent was to him a deliverance. Bettina was twenty-five and looked much younger. She was born in Frankfurt in 1785, the daughter of the beautiful Maximiliana La Roche, whom the young Goethe once loved, and of the merchant Brentano, who was twenty years older than her mother. The mother was a Protestant and a native of the Rhine Provinces; the father was a Catholic and of Italian origin. Her mother died when Bettina was eight, and her father when she was twelve. Educated first in a convent, and then among Protestants, she had always a mystical tendency, without, however, being able to connect it with any religion. Her brilliant natural gifts of art and poetry were tenderly nursed by one of her brothers, Clemens; in 1807 she formed a friendship with one of her brother's friends, the young nobleman and poet Achim von Arnim, whom she married in 1811. But the great event in her life was her passion for Goethe, which began in 1806 (of this I shall speak later on). She became the bosom friend of Goethe's mother, and through her she succeeded at last in meeting Goethe in 1807. From that moment she belonged to him until her death.

[10] Napoleon, who met her about the year 1809, asked, "Who is this fuzzy young person with fiery eyes?" (Draft of an unpublished letter by Bettina.)

We must not forget, as a background to our word-picture, the god of war and his conflagrations . . . Jena. . . . The year 1809 is crimson with the glare of blood-stained skies. In August, 1809, Bettina wrote to Goethe, "During the whole summer the flames of war have reddened my horizon."

[11] Alois Bihler, a student at the University of Landshut, was introduced into the family circle of Professor de Savigny, and there met Savigny's sister-in-law, Bettina. They spent part of the summer of 1810 together at Bukowan in Bohemia, on a property belonging to the Brentanos. Both were great music-lovers. Bihler taught Bettina harmony. The creative genius of this woman filled him with admiration: "She improvises poems while singing, and she sings while improvising, with a marvellous voice" (*"Singend dichtete sie und dichtend sang sie mit prachtvoller Stimme"*). "A magnificent contralto voice," wrote her granddaughter, Mme. Irene Forbes-Mosse. . . . A month after her meeting with Beethoven, on the 9th of July, Bettina wrote to Bihler, and this authentic letter is the most reliable basis on which we can build the story of this meeting. (See

Albert Leitzmann: *Beethoven und Bettina. Deutsche Revue*, February 1918.)

[12] On December 13, 1809, Wilhelm Grimm was lunching at Goethe's house, and was told by the latter that he had received Bettina's portrait by Louis Grimm (a beautiful picture which is reproduced in Fritz Bergemann's book); he praised it highly and expressed great joy. Wilhelm Grimm said that Bettina did not think the portrait very good. Goethe replied, "Yes, she is a dear child! Who could do justice to her? If Lucas Kranach were still alive, he would be equal to the task."

[13] In *Goethes Briefwechsel mit einem Kinde* (1835).

[14] " . . . A magnificent garden, full of flowers; all the glass houses were wide open; the scent of the flowers was overwhelming. . . . Beethoven stood in the burning sunshine, and said . . . " (May 28).

"A bunch of lilies of the valley fills my little room with its elusive perfume . . ." (May 15th).

And Beethoven's letter, perhaps not authentic (August), ". . . In our little observatory, during the splendid May rain, when I learned to know you . . ."

[15] In her letter to Bihler, she wrote *A Fantasy* . . . No doubt it was the *Sonata quasi una fantasia*, op. 27, no. 2 (*The Moonlight Sonata*).

[16] Her letter to Bihler describes both the house and the host: "In the first room, two or three pianos, without legs, on the floor; some chests, a rickety chair. In the second room, his bed: a straw mattress and a thin blanket; a wash basin on a deal table; his nightshirt is thrown on the floor." Beethoven kept her waiting; he was just shaving. (From this we can see that Bettina has embellished her entrance as described in her book published in 1835, quoted above.) He is small, dark, his face covered with pock marks, ugly but with a magnificent forehead—"a noble vault, a masterpiece!"—very long black hair which he brushed back. Much younger than his age, "one would take him to be not more than thirty"; he says he is thirty-five

and does not remember when he was born.—Within a quarter of an hour they are intimate friends.—He is sitting on the edge of a chair, by the piano, on which one of his hands is wandering softly. Then, suddenly, he forgets everythng round him; he is engulfed "in an ocean (*Weltmeer*) of harmony . . ." This whole account is of a life-like precision; we can feel that it was written under the immediate impression, with perfect spontaneity.

[17] The word "electricity" recurs often in her conversation with Beethoven.

[18] I have no wish to repeat here this magnificent conversation. It requires separate study and careful criticism. It abounds in flashes of genius, bursting through a cloud of mystical dreams, flashes which were generated in Bettina by that lonely visionary whom she had interrupted in the midst of his creative work. I shall limit myself to the undisputed facts.

[19] "*Heute war wieder übles Wetter*" ("The weather is bad again today"). Beethoven, in his grumbling way, made this sarcastic remark to Schindler, in the letter in which he broke off their relations in May, 1824.

[20] ". . . In all that concerns his art he is so sincere and so masterful (*herrschend*) that no other artist dares go near him. But in the other things of life he is so simple that people can do with him what they like. They laugh at him and his absent-mindedness; they take advantage of him; he rarely has enough money for his bare necessities. His friends and his brothers suck him dry (*aufzehren*). . . . His clothes are torn, his appearance is always tattered (*zerlumpt*). And yet he gives the impression of grandeur and majesty (*Seine Erscheinung is bedeutend und herrlich*). In his stubbornness he sees nothing of what is going on around him. While he is composing he is deaf to the world outside, his eyes are troubled, he is brimming with harmony, insensible to impressions from without; all ties between him and the rest of the world are broken, he lives in the profoundest solitude. If you speak to him at some length, and wait for an answer, he suddenly bursts into inarticulate sounds

(*er bricht plötzlich in Töne aus*), takes his paper and begins to write. His first step, when composing, is to sketch a vast plan, and it is on the basis of this plan that his work is shaped and controlled."

There is no need for me to dwell on the interest of such a description, which has never before been used by Beethoven's biographers. Bettina expresses herself here with perfect sincerity, and without a thought for the public, in the first impulse of her generous heart:

"Why do I write all this to you, in so much detail? Because I know that he is being wronged, because people are too mean to understand him, because I feel that I must describe him as he really is. . . . He is extremely kind to all who confide in him on musical matters, even to the weakest beginners. He is never tired of giving them advice and help, this man who is so jealous of his freedom. . . ."

[21] Bettina published three letters which Beethoven wrote to her: they are dated August 11, 1810, February 10, 1811, and July or August, 1812. The original of the second only has been found. This was fortunate for Bettina because otherwise the critics, who generally were ill-disposed towards her, would have declared that Beethoven's friendship for her existed only in her imagination. It so happens that her second letter is not the least affectionate of the three. As far as I am concerned I am not casting any doubt on the authenticity of the first letter which mentions intimate matters (an unhappy love affair) which Bettina could not have known from other sources. This letter is, besides, in typical Beethoven style. As for the third letter, the question is different. I shall speak of it later.

[22] Bettina's letter to Bihler.

[23] *So bricht er plötzlich in Töne aus* ("He suddenly bursts into sounds"). Bettina's letter to Bihler.

[24] In my other essay on Bettina in this book I shall show how at

a later stage in her political career she was a heroine of justice and the champion of all the oppressed.

[25] "*Ja, Dir möge ich alles sagen; es ist so viel und auch so wenig. . . . Alle Wahrheit ist dem Menschen zu schwer. . . . Was soll ich Dir sagen? der Du alles weist—und weist wie wenig die Worte dem innern Sinn gehorchen, dass sie ihn wahrhaft andeuten mögen . . .*" ("Yes, I would tell you everything; it is so much and yet so little. . . . All truth weighs so heavily on us human beings. . . . What am I then to tell you, who already know all? You know how powerless are words to convey the inner meaning").

[26] Literally: "The whole world rises and falls around him, as . . ." This enigmatic and curiously worded sentence becomes clear through the letter published in 1835, in which she enlarged on it: "*Das ganze menschliche Treiben geht wie ein Uhrwerk an ihm auf und nieder, er allein erzeugt frei aus sich das Ungeahnte, Unerschaffene . . .*" ("Just as the mechanism of a clock centres upon an axis, so does every form of human activity center upon him: he alone of himself, unchecked, brings to birth what has never before existed, the unimagined").

"*He alone.*" . . . It is as if Bettina, while writing the sentence in the original letter, felt instinctively that she could not write it to Goethe without offending him. So she left it unfinished.

[27] What did Goethe know of Beethoven in 1810? It seems that he had heard, for the first time, one of his works, on October 13, 1807. A young singer, Henrietta Hässler, of Erfurt, who wanted to become a member of his private choir (see my essay "Goethe the Musician") sang to Goethe "a scene by Beethoven." Probably this was a scene from *Fidelio* the first performance of which had taken place in November, 1805, and the second, in the revised form, in April, 1806.

[28] I have come to the conclusion that Beethoven's thoughts expressed by Bettina are not only far above Bettina's intelligence, but also far in advance of the spirit of the time, and that they represent the profoundest intuition of his creative genius. They certainly

emanate from Beethoven, but the impression which they made was far less clear in the young Bettina of 1810 than they became later, after long reflection, in the Bettina of 1835. An authentic letter from Bettina to Goethe (Christmas, 1810), full of her obscure and passionate thoughts on music, shows how her little head (*Köpfchen*) is constantly working since she left Beethoven. At the time the impression which she had received was far greater than her perception; only very gradually did she understand the fulness of the treasure over which she had brooded so long.

29 January 11, 1811.

30 Conversation with Councillor von Müller, January 26, 1825 (on the subject of Bettina).

31 In the *Briefwechsel* of 1835 Bettina imagines that Goethe writes an amiable answer to her first letter on Beethoven, and praises her in a fatherly way for what she told him of this great man; he carefully avoids expressing any judgment on Beethoven, but he mentions very politely the hope that he will meet him some day. All this is very probably an exact reflection of what Goethe said, but never wrote, to Bettina.

32 A hitherto unpublished document (a draft of a letter by Bettina), which I quote in the last essay in this book, page 171, proves that during these days at Teplitz this impression was not only platonic.

33 His autobiography.

34 Zelter had met Beethoven in Berlin in 1796; Beethoven, then twenty-six, had given several concerts there, especially at the *Singakademie,* when Zelter had been greatly impressed by his improvisations.

35 And at what a fatal moment! In September, 1812, just after the regrettable interview at Teplitz of which we shall speak later.

36 "*Nur die Toten sollen sie mir ruhen lassen und Beethoven* . . ." (Authentic letters from Bettina to Goethe, October 16th and November 4th, 1810.)

[37] In the remarkable letter of Christmas, 1810, which deserves a special note. I insert it as an appendix.

[38] This is not a literal translation, but it conveys the meaning: "*Ein recht beschränkter Eigensinn*" (An exceedingly stupid stubbornness).

[39] "*Wenn ich einen verlorenen Sohn hätte, so wollte ich lieber, er hätte sich von den Bordellen bis zum Schweinkoben verirrt, als dass er in den Narrenwust dieser letzten Tage sich verfüge; denn ich fürchte sehr, aus dieser Hölle ist keine Erlösung*" (letter to Reinhardt, quoted by Bergemann).

[40] He had told Bettina in his authentic letter of February 10, 1811, of his intention to do so, asking her to recommend him to Goethe. Bettina did so, and very warmly, though rather late, on the 11th of May, when Beethoven had already carried out his intention. But the dear girl was always lost in her dreams; days and weeks slipped by without her being aware of it. Let us remember, too, that just then she married (March 11th), and though this event was perhaps less important to her than her daydreams, it must surely have afforded her a certain distraction!

[41] The printing of the score was, however, delayed. Goethe received it only in January, 1812.

[42] *Das will alles umfassen und verliert sich darüber immer in's Elementarische, doch noch mit unendlichen Schönheiten im einzelnen.*

[43] "*Auf der Kippe stehen,*" a vernacular expression implying the disdain of the wise man for the child who continues at play, unaware of the coming fall.

[44] This authentic letter of the 11th of May, 1811, is a most valuable example of Bettina's way of editing texts. She gives Goethe Beethoven's message. She does not attempt to transcribe it word for word. She expresses exactly the meaning of the words, but at the same time she tries to give them the form which would produce the effect desired by Beethoven; we might say that she transposes Beethoven's words into the key of Goethe, and does all she can to win

Goethe over to the cause of Beethoven. Once more, then, she shows herself to be a true and devoted friend; knowing Goethe's weakness for adulation, she makes Beethoven say that he had composed his music to *Egmont*, for no other reason than that he loved him (Goethe), loved him with all his heart (*die ich aus Liebe, aus meiner Liebe zu ihm gemacht habe*). And she adds: "I will not speak evil of any man who calls himself your friend, though some do so from interested motives. But Beethoven is not one of these; his motives are quite unselfish. On him you have bestowed a great blessing; he has interpreted you with all the might of a free nature, he is a living witness of your overwhelming power."

She knew what she was saying, for she had heard the *Egmont* overture and raved over it: "*Seine Ouverture aus Egmont ist so herrlich dass ich sie das beste mögte nennen*" ("His overture to *Egmont* is so magnificent that I think it is the best music I ever heard"). I have no doubt that her letter was the determining cause of Goethe's cordial reply to Beethoven.

[45] Let us add that at Karlsbad he met Prince Lichnowsky and Prince Kinsky, Beethoven's protectors, and only such sponsors could persuade him to hold out his hand to the "peasant from the Danube."

[46] This can be seen from the awkward way in which he writes to Beethoven: His music has been mentioned to him by several people, with much praise. . . . He has never heard his music performed by artists and by distinguished amateurs without wishing that he could admire Beethoven himself at the piano, and enjoy his extraordinary talent. It almost seems that he looks upon Beethoven merely as a *virtuoso* of the piano. Yet the music to *Egmont* had been performed in Germany for over a year (the first performance was in Vienna on the 24th of May, 1810). Goethe knows nothing of it.

[47] On January 23rd, 1812, he makes the following entry in his diary: "*Abends, van Beethovens Musik zu Egmont*" ("In the evening Beethoven's music to *Egmont*"). And on the 20th of Feb-

ruary: "In the morning Herr von Boyneburg played Beethoven's composition to *Egmont.* He dined with us. After dinner, continuation of the music."

48 This was Christiana's spelling, as she pronounced the name.

49 Christiana, in her intimate effusions to her husband, used to address him as "My dear good Privy Councillor."

50 *Bettinas Leben und Briefwechsel mit Goethe,* by Fritz Bergemann. 1927.

51 "Zum Sehen geboren,	"I was born to see,
Zum Schauen bestellt	Destined to contemplate
. . . . .	. . . . .
Gefällt mir die Welt.	And I like this world.
. . . . .	. . . . .
Ihr glücklichen Augen,	Oh, ye happy eyes,
Was je ihr geseh'n,	Whatever you have seen,
Es sei wie es wolle,	Be it what it may
Es war doch so schön."	It was so beautiful!"

(Written in May, 1831, when Goethe was in his eighty-second year.)

52 This was not Christiana's fault. She was always her own simple, loyal, and outspoken self. Her recently published correspondence shows that she was lovable in spite of her vulgarity. Had she done nothing but inspire Goethe to write *Das Blümchen,* the modest and tender poem of 1813, which he gave her at their silver wedding, she would still be dear to Goethe's real friends. While she lived Goethe could rely on a steadfast affection. After she had gone he felt very lonely, very lost, in his domestic life. Behind the imposing façade of these last years was hidden great sadness and utter distress. His majestic mental balance was only resumed when he turned to his work, when he made his daily appearance before the world, when he was "on show." But how feeble he was in his private life, a weak-

ness of which his lucid mind was fully aware. Beethoven, like him supreme in his art, was no more master of his life than Goethe: his weakness seemed even more pronounced. He was less able to disguise it, and his character was more unbalanced. Beethoven was made of a tougher stuff, but the great man of Weimar was, after all, not the weaker of the two.

[53] Bettina's first letter, in which she revived the correspondence, was written on the 28th of July, 1817, after Christiana's death.

[54] She was the great-granddaughter of the Leonora d'Este whom Tasso immortalized.

[55] The Emperor Francis, the Empress of Austria, the Empress Marie-Louise of France, the King of Saxony, and a bevy of dukes and grand dukes—all the illustrious people of Germany and Austria.

[56] July 14, 1812. During these days Beethoven was exceptionally excited. It is quite possible that he had written the famous letter *To the Immortal Beloved* during the preceding week. Many facts taken together go to prove that the passionate encounter took place on the road between Prague and Teplitz.

[57] July 17, 1812: letter to little Emily M. of H., who had written him a complimentary letter.

[58] Goethe had arrived on the 14th.

[59] Others read the word *Zusammengerafter* (literally, "pulled together"), which is even more emphatic.

[60] It is exceedingly difficult to translate this, because the words are extraordinarily comprehensive. *Zusammengefasster,* and still more *Zusammengerafter*, convey the enormous tension of power to concentrate, while *inniger* describes "interior" depths of feeling. Goethe adds, "I understand why he needs must adopt an extraordinary attitude towards the world" (*"Ich begreife recht gut, wie er gegen die Welt wunderlich stehen muss"*). This, too, is an important admission by Goethe. (Letter to Christiana July 19, 1812.)

[61] One of them, from Bettina to Prince Pückler-Muskau, of 1832; the other from Beethoven to Bettina. They were published by her after both Beethoven and Goethe were dead. They seem to

be two similar versions of one and the same letter, and this has led to a controversy, as to which of the two gave rise to the other. However, to us one is as valuable as the other. It has been objected that at the end of Bettina's letter she mentions that immediately after the incidents which I shall describe later, Beethoven came *"to tell us all about it,"* and that this would have made unnecessary Beethoven's description of what happened, contained in his letter to Bettina, which was sent the next day. But *"us"* may mean, in Bettina's absence, her husband, Arnim, and her sister, Mme. de Savigny. And Beethoven, who was anxious to tell the story personally to Bettina, may have written to her on the next day. It is true that Beethoven's letter was addressed from Teplitz in August, 1812, whereas in August he was no longer in Teplitz, but in Karlsbad or Franzensbrunn, and that the quarrel at Teplitz occurred in July. But twenty years later, when Bettina found Beethoven's undated letter, she may have added one from memory, as she was accustomed to do. The presence of Archduke Rudolph during those days, which is mentioned in the letter (*"der Herzog Rudolf hat mir den Hut abgezogen"*)—"the Archduke Rudolf lifted his hat to me," has also been questioned. But here again it is possible that Bettina wished to complete Beethoven's letter, and in good faith filled in the name which he had left out. In any case, it is proved beyond all doubt—it has never, in fact, been contested—that she was in Teplitz at that time, and that Beethoven confided his trouble to her. Her testimony is of the greatest importance. I may add that of the two documents, Bettina's letter is more complete and tells us far more, although Beethoven's letter contains one of the finest sayings that he ever uttered. It would have required a second Beethoven to invent it.

[62] Goethe's diary.

[63] As soon as the news of the Arnims' arrival in Teplitz had reached her in Karlsbad, she wrote to her husband, insisting that he should not receive them. Goethe, in his reply of August 5th, with that domestic cowardice common to those who want peace at home at any

price, calmed his jealous wife by referring to the Arnims in most disrespectful terms.

[64] It is significant that Bettina's arrival and Beethoven's visit to her coincide with the latter's last meeting with Goethe. After July 23rd they never met again.

[65] Note the contemptuous meaning which Beethoven gives the word "romantic."

[66] Beethoven's letter to Bettina is couched in even stronger terms: "I told Goethe what a great effect discriminating approval has upon us, and how one longs to be heard with understanding by one's equal (*dass man von seines Gleichen mit dem Verstand angehört werden will*). Emotion is fit for womenfolk (forgive the words). But man—why, music must strike sparks from his mind (*Dem Mann muss Music Feuer aus dem Geiste schlagen*)."

We find the same contempt for sentimentality in his first conversation with Bettina in May, 1810. He thanked her for praising his music in terms which were without emotion, real or feigned. He is glad to hear her merry applause (*heiteren Beifall*). "Most people," says he, "are moved by something beautiful, but they are not artistically minded; artists burst into flames, not tears."

[67] Goethe shared this opinion. When in 1800 young Count Wolf Baudissin told him that for the sake of Bach he would be willing "to live, languish, and suffer," Goethe replied coldly, "In Art there is no such thing as suffering (*Von Leiden könne ja bei der Kunst keine Rede sein*)." This shows that in past days, he, in his turn, could have taught Beethoven a lesson. But his physical emotion often gave the lie to his reasoning. Tears would often rise to his eyes when he read aloud: then he would throw the book down angrily. He was annoyed at being so moved by the beauty of the passage. When Zelter, for the first time, played his *Lieder* in the presence of Goethe and Schiller, he was astounded to see the violent expression of their feeling. They "acted the Songs," marched up and down, gesticulating.

[68] I am following here the text of Bettina's letter to Pückler-

Muskau, which is not so well known as Beethoven's letter to Bettina. The latter is quoted, in part, in my short *Life of Beethoven.*

[69] This can be completed by Beethoven's letter to Bettina (it does not matter whether it was written by Beethoven himself or by Bettina from her notes of what he had told her).

"One must be what one would appear to be!" Beethoven is said to have told Goethe (*"Man muss sein was man scheinen will"*).

And he goes on: "I gave him a good talking-to, and showed him no mercy. I reproached him with all his sins, especially towards you, my dear Bettina."

This is a proof that Bettina had told Beethoven how vexed and grieved she was, and that this contributed to Beethoven's severity towards Goethe. Perhaps there is also a trace of jealousy in the following passage: "God! if only I could have had as good a time with you as that one (*wie der*) enjoyed. Believe me, I would have done greater, far greater things!"

The letter contains other interesting details which have since turned out to be correct and which are usually omitted. Goethe is shown coaching the empress in a theatrical part, and Beethoven refusing, in his grumbling fashion, to help with his music. We also see Goethe and his grand duke, enthusiastic (*verliebt*) over Chinese porcelain, and Beethoven, quaintly attributing this craze, which seemed to him absurd, to the unbalanced spirit of the time "in which reason has no longer the 'upper hand.' " Beethoven always quotes reason when he attacks Goethe. "But," he concluded, "I take no share in all these follies of theirs."

[70] With what keen intelligence did Goethe, who was not musical, appreciate the fact that Beethoven's musical powers were not affected by his deafness. He saw that the man only, not the artist, was stricken.

[71] The *sight*, not the *thought* of death. It goes without saying that a man of Goethe's intellectual and moral calibre never feared the *thought* of death. He often speaks of it, and we find many references to it in his *Conversations.* It will suffice to mention the

splendid *rêverie* prompted by the death of Wieland on January 25, 1813, and which Falk described at length. Generally speaking, Goethe set against the idea of entire dissolution his firm belief in the indestructibility of the spirit (among twenty other examples, see the conversation with Eckermann on May 2, 1824). "At the age of seventy-five, one is bound to think of death. This thought leaves me unperturbed because I am firmly convinced that our spirit is indestructible and progresses from eternity to eternity. . . ."

In considering death, it was not so much the idea of final annihilation which troubled him, as the strange conception that the surviving spiritual entity might be attacked by another grosser and more powerful spiritual being which would subjugate it. (See the conversation with Falk, in which Goethe, overwrought by his recent bereavement, abandoned his usual reserve on such subjects and spoke aloud to himself, as if hallucinated.)

What I am concerned with here is the repellent effect which the sight of death and of the dead always had on Goethe. This was a constant obsession of his, and there are many proofs of it. He himself spoke of it to Wilhelm von Humboldt: "*Daher sehe ich keine Toten*" ("That is why I will not look on any dead man"), December 3, 1808. He gives all kinds of poetical reasons for this. He compares life to light. When life has departed, when the sun has set, there remains only "*das Grau des Stoffes* (the greyness of substance)." His reason for refusing to see in death those whom he knew in life is that if he were to look upon their bodies he would feel that they were for ever "*verblichen und verschwunden* (faded and vanished)."

This explanation is no doubt correct, but it is partial: it does not give us all that was in his subconscious mind. But whatever the reason may be, the fact remains that Goethe avoided the spectacle of death. In *Goethe*, by Emil Ludwig, there is an account of the death of one of Goethe's friends, the Minister of State von Voigt, and the tender, poignant letter of the dying man; twenty-four hours later he was dead, just a few steps from Goethe's house.

Goethe, who lacked the courage to visit him, had calmly replied to his letter. . . . Another who well knew his aversion to death was Frau von Stein. On her deathbed she gave instructions that her funeral was not to pass before her good friend's house. During the funeral Goethe stayed at home, reading Victor Hugo and *Hunting in Mongolia*. . . . But when an intimate friend came to describe the ceremony, he burst into tears.

Let us not, therefore, be hard in our judgment. Do not let us accuse him of lack of feeling. Who has ever explored the depth of his sorrows? Let us rather read once more the immortal plaint, in *Wilhelm Meister*, of the Harpist.

[72] At the age of eighty, he said, "*Wollte ich mich ungehindert gehen lassen, so läge es wohl in mir, mich selbst und meine Umgebung zu Grunde zu richten* (If I were to let myself go, without restraint, I should bring to utter ruin not only myself, but all those near and dear to me)."

[73] "*Was euch nicht angehört, müsset ihr meiden, was euch das Innere stört, dürft ihr nicht leiden*" (You must shun what does not concern you: you *cannot* endure that which disturbs your inner self)."

[74] Let us add that Goethe at that time was flirting assiduously with the first lady-in-waiting, Countess O'Donnell, and was very busy writing her love letters and poems.

[75] Letter to Breitkopf, August 9, 1812.

[76] *Und freute sich ganz kindisch dass er Goethen so geneckt habe.*

[77] They were not alone in this. At that time Goethe was showing an exaggerated respect for those in high position, and their victories. He had just praised the Empress of France and the continental blockade. German patriots rose in revolt against this, and popular irony avenged itself by calling Goethe's wife "*Frau Abstinentalrätin.*"

[78] When he returned to his home in Weimar he found Zelter's rude letter which was so insulting to Beethoven, and which I have

mentioned already (see page 24). Considering Goethe's disposition, it must have had a deadly effect on him.

[79] It was this likeness which fetched out the old bear from the solitude of his woods. "The wild man" (*der wilde Mann*) who refused all invitations came and played for Rahel one afternoon, but it was the deaf playing to the deaf; music meant very little to her.

[80] This remark was made by Kalischer (*Beethoven und Berlin*). I have, however, found it to be correct by comparing it with Rahel's writings, and was all the more surprised at it because she frequently mentions music and musicians, with the single exception of Beethoven. On the other hand her husband, Varnhagen, to whom she is the Law and the Prophets, expressed, up to 1812, a boundless admiration for Beethoven (letter to Uhland, 1811). From 1812 on he too is obediently silent. He stands aside and mentions him only in passing.

[81] But he is still unaware that Beethoven had written other music also to this work.

[82] On January 29, 1814, *Egmont* was at last performed with music for the first time in Weimar. Goethe enters in his diary, "In the evening, *Egmont*. . . ."

He did not mention Beethoven's name.

Again, while he spoke at length in his letters of the pleasure which he derived from Himmel's insignificant music to his *Lieder*, or from the compositions of titled nonentities like Count von Dietrichstein, Beethoven never received a single word of appreciation or blame, which he so ardently desired. It is also significant that while his correspondent, F. von Gentz, who sent him Dietrichstein's *Lieder*, added much praise of Beethoven's three beautiful *Lieder* to poems by Goethe, which were published at that time, Goethe in his reply praised the titled musician's work profusely and ceremoniously, but never so much as mentioned Beethoven's.

[83] Where was the discovery made? He found his road to Damascus—oh, bitter irony!—in the weakest of Beethoven's compositions, the only wretched rhapsody among all that he wrote, the *Schlacht-*

symphonie, 1816 ("The Battle of Vittoria"). On hearing it, Zelter became greatly excited, threw his perruque in the air, and shouted: "Vivat Genius! And may the devil take all the critics! (*und hol' der Teufel alle Kritik!*)" Nor was this all. The same ironical fate decreed that at the close of his life Zelter should go into raptures over the same "scandalous" *Christ on the Mount of Olives*, which he had described as being "pervertedly lustful." In 1831 this "shameless" work of old had become "soothing and charming, like the pleasant dream of a summer night."

[84] Marianna, who for two years had been a dancer, singer, and comédienne, at the theatre in Frankfurt, before marrying in 1814 the rich banker Willemer, twenty-four years older than herself; she was both poetess and musician; she was a good exponent of Mozart's *Lieder*, and had a profound understanding of the fine influence of music, and of the relief it brings in sorrow—"*was du erlebst in dir erneut und mild dir's nur gewährt, so dass was schwarzte, sich verklärt, was freute inniger erfreut.*" . . . "Music . . . gives new and milder forms to one's feelings, makes bright what was dark, and increases the joy of what is pleasant."

[85] June 26, 1821.

[86] July 12, 1821.

[87] His intuition of the music of the future is remarkable. One is not surprised to find that Lobe became one of the foremost German theoreticians of the next period.

[88] "That is the evil spirit which threatens you young fellows! You are ever ready to create new ideals, but how do you carry them into effect? Your principle, that each part in music must express something, sounds very well. Yes, it seems as if it should have been recognized and practised long before by every composer, because it is sound reason. But whether the musical work of art lends itself to the use of this principle, and whether the enjoyment of music does not suffer through it, is a different question. You would do well not to be satisfied merely with thinking this out, but to experiment with it. In every form of art there are certain weaknesses connected with

the fundamental idea, which must be allowed for in practice, because if we disregard them we come too close to nature, and our art becomes inartistic (*unkünstlerisch*)."

This lesson of a master artisan is worthy of consideration. The inventors of theories on art, the "ists" of all times, would do well to take it to heart. Certainly no theory has any value unless proved in practice. But Goethe's practical tests were far too hasty, and as far as the present instance is concerned, were certainly biassed.

89 On principle, Goethe was resolutely opposed to "speech with music"—to "melodrama"—and he said so on many occasions. See his conversation with W. von Humboldt, on December 3, 1808:

"*Gegen das Sprechen zur Musik erklärte sich Goethe so: Musik sei die reine Unvernunft und die Sprache habe es nur mit der Vernunft zu thun* (Music has nothing whatever to do with reason, while speech has to do with nothing but reason)." He referred to Schiller's bad habit of demanding music to accompany his speeches, as in the *Maid of Orléans*, but added that he, Goethe, had always been against it. Humboldt heard him on many occasions speak strongly on the same matter. (We shall return to this subject, which is well worth discussing; Goethe did not mean to deprive himself of music, but wanted to incorporate it in poetry which, as he said, was to him a superior kind of music. See Essay III in this book, "Goethe the Musician.") Goethe's admission in public, that the composer had "admirably understood his meaning" in *Egmont's* monologue was in any case no small victory for Beethoven.

90 It is he who gave the Sonata, op. 27, no. 2, the name "Moonlight Sonata."

91 "The Councillor of State of Weimar, Schmidt, an ardent admirer of Beethoven, played all his sonatas with much fire and facility (*sic*). He knew many of them by heart" (Rellstab).

92 According to Max Friedlaender it was the manuscript of *Wonne der Wehmut.*

[93] Frimmel, *Beethovenstudien, II.*

[94] Goethe had made a note, on May 21, 1822, that he had received them, and though he was so particular in matters of courtesy, he had no word of thanks for Beethoven.

[95] Theodore de Wyzewa, *Beethoven and Wagner.* The article on Beethoven and Goethe is puerile and full of mistakes.

[96] "The poor fellow is almost completely deaf. I could hardly restrain my tears."

When in 1825 Zelter wrote to Beethoven, through Rellstab, who conveyed the letter, "it was written," said Rellstab, "in terms such as might be addressed to a saint in heaven." Beethoven was much moved by this, and deeply thankful.

[97] We cannot find any reference either in Rahel's profuse correspondence, which included all the intellectual and artistic horizon of Europe. We ought to make a list of those great German personalities of the time, for whom Beethoven's death had no significance. And yet Beethoven's death created a considerable stir. The popular apotheosis on the occasion of Beethoven's funeral in Vienna reëchoed triumphantly throughout the world.

[98] July 24, 1809.

[99] According to a note in his letter to Humboldt, Goethe's "*Helena, klassisch-romantische Phantasmagorie, ein Intermezzo zu Faust . . .*" was published during this year. This arbitrary interpolation of an episode in *Faust* almost "deforms" the great work.

[100] Goethe was evidently thinking of the orchestra performing the piece which Mendelssohn had played to him. But his astonishment gives his thoughts an extraordinary form. It is as if humanity as a whole was drawn into the whirlwind of the C Minor Symphony.

[101] I have come to this conclusion by several different paths in the course of writing this essay.

[102] In the Conversation Notebook we see that after the visitor had left, Beethoven complained to Schindler of what he had said.

[103] Beethoven's memory is here at fault; he should have said

"Teplitz." This is a further reason why Bettina must be excused when she gave the letter received from Beethoven in Teplitz the date of August instead of July, 1812.

[104] December, 1826.

[105] It was to Hummel that he addressed the two well-known notes, written one after the other in 1798:

"Don't come to me again!" (Beethoven here used the third person, which at that time was used in Germany when speaking to a subordinate.) "You are a treacherous hound: the dog-catcher should be after you."

"Dear friend of my heart! (*Herzens Nazerl!*) You are a loyal fellow, and you were right; I can see it now. So please come to me this afternoon. You will meet also Schuppanzigh and between the two of us we are going to give you a good roughing, pommelling and shaking (*rüffeln, knüffeln und schütteln*), to your heart's content.

"I hug you. Your Beethoven, alias 'Flour Basin' (*Mehlschöberl*) *."

[106] In 1829, speaking to Eckermann, Goethe went so far as to compare Hummel to Napoleon. "Napoleon controls the world as does Hummel his piano. The two seem to us admirable in their mastery; how each contrives to do it we cannot tell, and yet it is so, and it has happened under our very eyes." April 7th.

[107] "I could hardly restrain my tears" (letter to Goethe, September 14, 1819). In this letter Zelter refers to the extraordinary respect in which Beethoven was held in Vienna, in spite of all the criticism of his strange character. This testimony of high public esteem over Zelter's signature could not fail to impress Goethe, the Privy Councillor.

[108] What are we to think of Rochlitz's silence, when he wrote to Goethe, describing his voyage, without even mentioning Beethoven? Many of Goethe's visitors had been directly or indirectly in touch with Beethoven—Louis Spohr, Emmanuel Alois Förster, etc.

* TRANSLATOR'S NOTE.—*Mehlschöberl* in Viennese dialect means "Flour Basin" and is a nickname often given to stout persons.

[109] "*. . . Mir ist das All, ich bin mir selbst verloren,*
Der ich noch erst den Göttern Liebling war.
. . . .
Sie trennen mich, und richten mich zu Grunde."

("The world is lost to me, and lost my inner self,
And yet I was once the darling of the gods.
. . . .
They sever me, and ruin me")
—*Elegie von Marienbad.* Summer, 1823.

[110] When, later in life, he remembered this, he wept once more.

[111] "*Nun aber doch das eigentlich Wunderbarste! Die ungeheure Gewalt der Musik auf mich in diesen Tagen! Die Stimme der Milder, das klangreiche der Szymanowska, ja sogar die öffentlichen Exhibitionen der hiesigen Jägerkorps, falten mich auseinander wie man einen geballte Faust freundlich flach lässt*" ("And now the most wonderful thing of all! The enormous power which music has had over me lately! Milder's voice, Szymanowska's playing, even the public performances of the local infantry band—they all make me relax just as a man's fist, closed in anger, opens under a friendly impulse.")

[112] Maria Szymanowska, *née* Wotowska, was born in 1790. She died, still a young woman, in 1832, the same year as Goethe, at St. Petersburg.

Was her musical talent outstanding? I have been fortunate in acquiring a private edition of her compositions, not mentioned by Eitner and Fétis. *Twenty Exercises and Preludes for Pianoforte, composed and dedicated to Countess Chodkiewick by Mme. Szymanowska,* née *Wotowska, First Edition, 47 engraved pages.* These compositions are written in a fluent but somewhat nebulous style, which was no doubt the result of the influence of Field, whose pupil she had been, although both were almost the same age. Her style was, in a way, a forerunner of Mendelssohn, with here and there a touch of Schumann. The part for the right hand is light and graceful, that for the left hand is rudimentary only. It is characteristic that out of twenty pieces there is not a single one which is passionate or pathetic, *allegro molto* or *adagio*. Nearly all of them are a milder kind—*moderato, scherzando, grazioso, con spirito, commodo*. The only one which attempts to express "thought" or which, to use a simpler expression, approaches emotion, is the last, *cantabile*, where to our surprise we find a passage reminding us of an orchestral arrangement from *Fidelio* (*O Gott! Welch ein Augenblick!*). Ariel's fingers do not trouble the old heart, too exposed to emotion and too fearful of it: they lull it to rest.

[113] Some one had proposed the toast, "Our memories." Goethe knocked on the table and said (the following is a short summary of his words): "I do not like these words. The toast seems to imply that we have forgotten and that some outer event recalls our memories to us. Those things which are great and beautiful never leave us; they become part of ourselves; they bring forth in us a new and better 'ego': thus they go on living and creating within ourselves. It is not the past but the eternally new which our desires would have us seek; the new is itself the creation of ever-growing elements of the past. True longing (*die echte Sehnsucht*) must always be productive (*produktiv*) and fashion a new and better self. . . . And," he adds, "this is precisely what we have felt during these last days. Our deepest, inmost self has been refreshed, refined, ennobled, by this glorious artist. No, she can never leave us, for she has passed into our most intimate selves and will for ever live within us. . . ."

[114] Hiller gave an account of this later in his book, *Aus dem Tonleben unserer Zeit, neue Folge 1868-71* (Contemporary Musical Notes. New Series).

[115] Hummel was so full of Beethoven's greatness that when in 1830 he organized a series of concerts at popular prices at the Hoftheater in Weimar, he inaugurated them with the overture to *Leonora* and the *Battle of Vittoria.*

[116] The following is a definite indirect proof: J. J. Ampère and

Albert Stapfer called on Goethe about this time (the end of March or the beginning of April). They would also have liked to see Weimar's second celebrity, Hummel (these were their own words). But Hummel was still away.

"The latter, for whom we also had a letter of introduction, had left for Vienna, to delight the ears of the Austrian public, and we hope very much that we shall meet him there. We have been . . . very disappointed at missing him. . . ."

Not a word of Beethoven. Nobody in Weimar told them. Goethe, who knew it, did not tell them that Beethoven was dying and that Hummel had gone to close his eyes. This concealment seems horrible to me.

[117] Since January 29, 1814.

[118] I have in my collection a call-sheet of the Hoftheater in Weimar, signed "*Goethe*," dated September 19, 1816, in which we read:

Monday, September 23rd: *Nathan.*

Tuesday, September 24th: Rehearsal of *Griselda.*
Afternoon, general rehearsal of *Fidelio.*

Wednesday, September 25th: Performance of the Opera *Fidelio.*

This was two years after the performances in Vienna.

[119] Why should he have deprived himself of one of his mental powers? He needed them all.

"Are we to give first place to the historian or to the poet? This question should never be asked. They are not rivals, any more than the runner and the wrestler. Each deserves his laurel crown" (*Gedanken in Prosa,* part IV, 1825).

[120] He was fond of quoting the French saying: "Voir venir les choses est le meilleur moyen de les 'expliquer.' "

[121] Rochlitz intended to organize in Weimar a much more important series of lectures, with musical illustrations, dealing with the five principal periods of musical history in Germany and Italy,

during the preceding three centuries. The cholera epidemic of 1831 prevented this plan from being carried out.

[122] Even when we revert to the great works of the past (and each period selects different works from that great library: yesterday, Beethoven and Wagner; to-day, Bach and Mozart) it is never the past which comes to life in us; it is we ourselves who cast our shadows on the past, with our desires, our problems, our sense of order or our confused thinking. The Bach of our day has nothing in common with the Bach of Goethe's day, not to speak of Bach himself. We can never hope to penetrate the inner self of others.

[123] The standard work on this subject is that mine of information, *Die Tonkunst in Goethes Leben*, 2 vols., by Wilhelm Bode. Berlin, 1912, (*Music in Goethe's life*), completed by the same author's other work *Goethes Schauspieler und Musiker,* 1 vol. Berlin. 1912. (*Goethe's Actors and Musicians.*)

There is nothing in Goethe's life which Bode does not know, but Bode is not a musician. The same subject, however, has been treated from the musician's point of view by Hermann Abert, an eminent writer on music, in his excellent work, *Goethe und die Musik* (J. Engelhorn's Nachf. Stuttgart, 1922). The principal feature of this little book is the reconstruction of the musical atmosphere in which Goethe lived; the author shows clearly to what extent Goethe agreed with the ideas of the time on music in general and on the different forms of music, *Lied*, opera, and instrumental music, and in what way his art reacted upon the music of his time, and *vice versa.*

I must also mention the writings on this subject by Wasielewsky, Philip Spitta, and Max Friedlaender.

[124] *Seine Freude am Klange.*

[125] The actor Genast, in his memoirs, shows him forbidding the public to laugh at a performance of *Ion* in 1802, and calling to order rowdy students of Jena at a performance of Schiller's *Räuber* (*The Robbers*) in 1808. Here is another amusing anecdote, told by the music historian, Christian Lobe (*vide* his conversation with

Goethe, pages 58 and 59 of this book). Lobe was then young, and very much in love with an actress who was playing in *Turandot* at Weimar. He had slipped into a dark corner of the theatre during the rehearsal, and tried to watch her from behind a column. But as she was on his side of the stage he could not see her. Lobe came out from his hiding-place, and from seat to seat worked his way to the centre of the stalls. He saw his beloved, she saw him, and the silly young lovers exchanged signs of recognition. Lobe, in his joy, rose, without thinking, from his seat. Suddenly, from the depth of a box, thundered the bass voice of His Excellency von Goethe, "Remove that dirty mongrel from my sight!" (*"Schafft mir doch den Schweinehund aus den Augen!"*) Lobe fled, jumping over the seats, stumbling, falling, in utter confusion and shame, with the laughter of the actors ringing in his ears. Only long after did he hear that Goethe's vigorous remark was not addressed to him, but to the coach and accompanist, Eilenstein, a drunkard, who was strumming on the piano a fantastic march which had derived its inspiration from the bottle.

126 Like Beethoven, he composed many of his poems as he walked and sang, and there is a good reason why a number of them have the title "The Wanderer." A significant passage in the *Wanderjahre* ("Years of Wandering") of *Wilhelm Meister* reveals to us the musical character of his creative process:

"It often happens that a hidden genius whispers a rhythm to me, so that, as I wander about, I am always moving to it. I hear faint sounds, too, the accompaniment of a *Lied* which somehow pleasantly suggests itself to me." (*"Mir scheint oft ein geheimer Genius etwas Rhythmisches vorzuflüstern, so dass ich mich beim Wandern jedesmal im Takt bewege und zugleich leise Töne zu vernehmen glaube, wodurch denn irgendein Lied begleitet wird, dass sich mir auf eine oder die andere Weise gefällig vergegenwärtigt"*) *III. I.*

Thus, it is first the rhythm which forms the framework, then the melody which clothes it. Finally there is the poem itself. Abert correctly states that the rhythm is the soul of the "inner music" from which Goethe's poems have sprung. *"Der Takt kommt aus der poetischen Stimmung, wie unbewusst"* ("The rhythm is the unconscious outcome of the poetical mood") (to Eckermann April 6th, 1829).

[127] Bode, op. cit., II, 345.

[128] *"Meine Seele löst sich nach und nach durch die lieblichen Töne aus den Banden der Protokolle und Akten"* ("Pleasant musical sounds gradually set my soul free from the bonds of juridical protocols and acts") (February 22, 1779). After his almost fatal illness of 1801 his first desire was to hear music.

[129] During the Seven Years' War the French were in occupation of Frankfurt for four years. Their theatrical companies came from Paris.

[130] Gluck's importance for Goethe, as for Herder and Klopstock, depended not only upon his beautiful and classic construction of a tragedy set to music with choruses, which called to mind the old Greek tragedies, but also upon the happy enunciation which he secured of the music latent in poetical speech. His small collection of *Lieder* written to Klopstock's odes and particularly that very short masterpiece *"Die frühen Gräber"* ("The Graves of the Young") was an unsurpassed model for all the German artists of the period. He thus showed the poets the way to a *Sprachmelodie* ("melodic speech"), a melody of the word, a musical poetry. It is difficult to realize nowadays what a fountain of study these short odes, so soberly clad in music, were for the greatest writers of that generation in Germany.

[131] On May 6, 1776, while in the mountains near Ilmenau, he wrote his *"Rastlose Liebe"* ("Restless Love").

[132] A fine letter from Wieland to Gluck, written on June 13, 1776, tells us of his attempts to approach Goethe, who alone was worthy to write such a work, and the unfortunate circumstances which prevented his plan from being carried out. . . . "I went to see him and showed him your letter. I found him next day already

full of a great scheme on this subject; I could see it taking shape, and was delighted with it, notwithstanding the great difficulties. But nothing seems impossible to Goethe. I saw how lovingly he tended it. Give him but a few days of peace and solitude and what I read in his soul would become a reality. . . . But Fate granted neither him nor you this consolation. . . . His situation here became continually more and more difficult, and his activity was distracted in other directions. . . . In short, there is now practically no hope that he will in the near future complete the work which he began. He certainly did not abandon it of his own free will. I know that from time to time he is still seriously working at it; but what can one expect when, on account of his many duties, he has not a single day he can call his own? However, knowing this great mortal (*den herrlichen Sterblichen*) as I do, I feel certain that he will complete it yet . . ."

133 May 25, 1776.

134 It has been suggested that it was the first sketch of his *Proserpina.*

135 I have collected quite a number of documents bearing on this tragic event in Gluck's life. Among these original letters is one from "the little Chinese girl" to Abbé Arnaud, which I think is unique, and also the moving letter from Gluck to Klopstock, written on May 10, 1776, two weeks after his niece's death.

136 In the grand-ducal library at Weimar there is a magnificent bust of Gluck, purchased by the grand duke directly from the sculptor Houdon, in Paris, in 1775.

137 His letters to Kayser, 1785-86, show how thoroughly he had studied Gluck, his operas, and his *Lieder.*

138 Diary. May 13, 1780-January 7, 1781.

139 He had them sung by his private choir.

140 He shared the same taste with Herder in Weimar.

141 For the tercentenary of the Reformation, October 31, 1817.

142 To Karl Gottlieb Freudenberg, 1825.

143 We cannot understand, however, why he did not try to col-

laborate with him. No doubt on account of his friendship with Kayser. It was one of the characteristics of this great artist always to sacrifice art to friendship if the two were in conflict.

[144] The auditorium of the theatre had been burnt out in 1774, shortly before Goethe's arrival (1775). The company was disbanded and an entirely fresh start had to be made. It was a thankless task, especially as far as music was concerned.

[145] It is interesting to note that since 1795 Goethe had intended to write a sequel to the *Magic Flute*, the value of which he defended against the criticism of most of his friends. In 1798 Effland encouraged him to do it, but Schiller dissuaded him. He published a fragment of it. As late as 1801 he mentioned it to Zelter as a musical poem. Abert, who analysed the fragment, thinks that it is preparatory to the second *Faust* and considers that of all of Goethe's poems this is the most suitable for interpretation by music in its most varied forms, from tragedy in the style of Gluck to the German ballad opera (*Singspiel*). The chorus plays an independent part. Simple prose is mingled with free rhythm in rhyme.

[146] Nevertheless, in 1827 he regretted that he could not derive the same pleasure as before from hearing the *Magic Flute*.

[147] Eckermann, unfortunately, had no one better to suggest than Rossini, and Goethe, on the other hand, proposed Meyerbeer! Beethoven's name was not mentioned, even as a regretful afterthought. Yet we know that to write the music to *Faust* was one of Beethoven's ardent desires, and that Goethe's friend Rochlitz had been asked by the publisher Breitkopf to propose the poem to Beethoven in 1822.

[148] Goethe died on March 22nd.

[149] Gluck was given only very rarely, in spite of Goethe's wish. *Iphigenie auf Tauris* was performed in 1800, and *Armida* in 1832.

[150] June 24, 1826. "Every day I am fonder of music which excites (*das Aufregende*)," he had written forty years previously, in 1787, during his travels in Italy, where the sugary sentimentality of the *Opera Seria* bored him.

[151] November 9, 1829.

[152] His pupil, Johann Kasper Vogler, was organist in Weimar for forty-four years, until 1765.

[153] In 1800. I have described this conversation on page 218.

[154] Eduard Genast, *"Aus Weimars Klassischer und Nachklassischer Zeit"* (Weimar's classical and post-classical period).

[155] March 11, 21, and April 17, 1828. Soon after these great performances, Mendelssohn came to spend two weeks in Weimar. He spoke of them to Goethe and played some excerpts to him. Goethe was delighted to find that, contrary to what had happened in the case of Mozart, his taste for Bach's music had not weakened. He listened to Mendelssohn "with pleasure, interest, and reflection" (1830).

[156] "It almost seems," wrote Zelter, "as if the whole ensemble were an organ each pipe of which is endowed with intelligence, energy, and will power, without mannerisms and without being forced, in any way (*Zwang*)."

[157] Bach's music makes him think of God in the Book of Genesis. His fine saying is well known: *"Als wenn die ewige Harmonie sich mit sich selbst unterhielte, wie sich's etwa in Gottes Busen, kurz vor der Weltschöpfung möchte zugetragen haben"* (It is as if the Eternal Harmony soliloquized, as must have happened in God's bosom just before the Creation) (Correspondence with Zelter, II, 95. Reclam edition).

[158] "Man's self, in so far as he employs his healthy senses, is the most powerful and the most accurate physical apparatus in existence" (Letter of 1808 to Zelter, to which I shall refer again later). Goethe invariably opposes the tenets of mathematicians and physicians which suggest a dependence on artificial instruments without regard to the living man, the most perfect of all instruments.

[159] Goethe was delighted to hear that Bach's contemporaries were amazed at the skill and agility of his legs at the organ, a fact which supported his own theory. Zelter, poking fun at the mania of

the great man, his friend, on this subject, said, "Without feet Bach would never have reached the height of his genius."

[160] He corresponded with the philologist, Friedrich A. Wolf, on the subject of Greek music.

[161] 1808.

[162] On the other hand, in 1810 Zelter gave him a lecture on Palestrina's *Missa Papae Marcelli.*

[163] I have already remarked how often excessive scruples of friendship, much as they were to his honour, harmed him intellectually.

[164] Between 1824 and 1832 he read a number of books and treatises on music, notably those of Rochlitz on the subject of the fugue, the origins of opera, on church music from the days of Orlando Lasso and so on. He read carefully the musical journals, particularly the *Caecilia* of Gottfried Weber.

Nor must we forget the importance which he attaches to the schoolmaster's rôle in music. In *Wilhelm Meister's Years of Wandering* (II, 1), music is at the root of all instruction. It is the central point from which all roads diverge: exercises of the hand, the ear, the eye, writing, arithmetic, etc.

[165] He mentions them in his letters 1829-31.

[166] *Festschrift zu R. V. Liliencron's 90 Geburtstage.*

[167] He returned to it in 1831.

[168] 1808.

[169] Compare the definition of the minor in his *Prose Thoughts,* Part VII: "The minor mode is the harmony of passionate desire. The desire which aspires to what is far off but which concentrates melodiously within itself, produces the minor mode" (*"Die Sehnsucht die nach aussen, in die Ferne strebt, sich aber melodisch in sich selbst beschränkt, erzeugt den Minor"*) (*Nachlass*).

[170] For a solution of this musical puzzle I have resorted to the kindly erudition of the two undoubted experts on the history of the songs of the people in France and Germany—M. Julien Tiersot, the historian of Rouget de Lisle, and Professor Max Friedlaender,

who has nothing to learn on the subject of the German *Volkslied* in the eighteenth and nineteenth centuries. The exact information which they have been good enough to afford me makes Beethoven's silence still more remarkable.

In an appendix to this book will be found a brief history of the *Marseillaise* in Germany, where it became immediately well known, though its significance was curiously misunderstood.

171 February 19, 1815. This impression clearly echoes that which Goethe directly received at Mainz twenty-two years before, and which he recorded in his story of the siege after the French garrison had marched out. "The most remarkable scene, and the one which struck all of us, was the appearance of the light cavalry. They advanced upon us in complete silence; suddenly their band struck up the *Marseillaise.* There is something mournful and threatening in this *Te Deum* of the Revolution even when it is played in lively fashion. On this occasion, however, it was played very slowly in time to their slow pace. The effect was terrible and awe-inspiring" (from Porchat's French translation).

172 At which Zelter, who had never considered the matter at all, cried in astonishment, "You and he (*Le Neveu de Rameau*) understand music better than I."

173 It seems that he heard a piece by Beethoven for the first time five months later.

174 1831.

175 The strange letter from Bettina to Goethe, about Christmas, 1810, which I translate in an appendix to this book, is further evidence.

176 Goethe, a year old when Jean Sebastian Bach died, and ten years old when Handel died, was born the same year as Cimarosa. He was twenty-five when Jommelli died, forty-two when Mozart died, and sixty the year of Haydn's death. But he was twenty-seven years of age when Weber was born, forty-eight when Schubert was born, and fifty-four in the year of Berlioz's birth.

177 In the *Lieder* in which the music is written under his dictation,

if one may so express it, he insists that the music should follow the minutest details in the text, the divisions into verses and strophes, the punctuation and the declamation. When the poem contains several strophes he must have the same melody for each; it is the singer's business to vary the expression. In 1822 again, speaking of a setting by Tomaschek, of his *Kennst du das Land*, which he likes, he expresses his displeasure with Beethoven and Spohr, who have disregarded his instructions with regard to the return of the melody with each strophe. Where he has written "*Lied,*" he will not allow it to be turned into an "*Aria.*"

[178] I too have heard Clara Schumann speak of the old Goethe who raised her higher on her chair, so that her baby hands could reach the keys. May I not say that I have seen Goethe?

[179] This curious passion for libretti persisted till his very last years. In 1828 he amused himself by rewriting the libretto for Rossini's *Moses*. He wanted to rewrite his *Tancredi* in the form of a *favola boscareccia* in the fashion of Poussin. A month before his death, in February, 1832, he dictated a long essay on the poems of Jouy, the librettist of Spontini. He was enthusiastic over Handel's verse, and could not forgive Weber those of *Euryanthe* and *Oberon*. Here Beethoven shared his views; in the eyes of both the best opera libretto was that of *The Water Carrier* of Cherubini.

He would never judge an opera independently of the words. The words must always be the first consideration.

"I don't understand you, my friends," he said in 1828. "How can you possibly separate the subject from the music and enjoy one without regard to the other? I marvel at you. How can the hearing contrive to appreciate the pleasures of harmony, when the sight, most powerful of the senses, is tortured by the imbecility of the subject. . . ."

Instead of sight he might well have said reason, and reason is the subject of the rest of the homily. But as a matter of fact the eye was, with Goethe, the organ of reason.

He was right. Most musicians possess very poor sight, and still less reason. We do not blame them for it, so long as their ears are long. But there is nothing to compel them to put their music into operas, that is to say to torture both sight and common sense. I cordially approve Goethe's sentiments, and Beethoven I know would have cried, "Bravo."

[180] The most curious of these musical works of his early youth is a *Concerto Dramatico composto dal Sigr. Dottore Flamminio, detto Panurgo Secondo*, written at Frankfurt in the autumn of 1772. (It may be found on pp. 77-82. Vol. III, of *Der Junge Goethe*, Max Morris edition, 1910, Inselverlag.) This "concerto," the word being used in the old meaning of "cantata," was composed "for performance in the *Gemeinschaft der Heiligen*, at Darmstadt." It is a ludicrous succession of pieces which are given musical titles, with expression and tempo marks: *Tempo giusto C, Allegretto 3/8 Arioso, Allegro con furia, Cantabile, Lamentabile; ein wenig geschwinder con speranza, Allegro con spirito, Choral, Capriccio con variazioni 1, 2, 3; Air Français, Molto andante, Con expressione*, and, to end up, *Presto fugato* with a double choir imitating in burlesque fashion the sounds of the instruments: "Dum du, dum du. Dum dim di di du (bis) Hohu! Hohu! . . .

[181] December 29, 1779.

[182] January 20, 1780.

[183] Abert has analysed these libretti and has made a list of the many and varied forms of aria, ensemble, and chorus. He shows that Goethe had a remarkable knowledge of every kind of theatrical music of his time, French, Italian and German.

[184] Meanwhile Goethe heard at Weimar and in Italy (September 3, 1786—June 18, 1788) a number of Italian *opere buffe* by Goldoni, Piccinni, Salieri, and Cimarosa. He drank them in; he revised and rearranged his old *Singspiele* in the light of his new experience of the Italian stage. He even intended to put his *Scherz, List und Rache* into Italian. German now seemed to him a *barbarische Sprache* to set to music. Ah! had he only known twenty years ago what he knows today. He would have made a study of Italian so as to write

for the lyric stage. He had another reason for his preference for Italian, and a very singular one, the need which he felt for the employment of a foreign language, Italian or Latin, to represent remarkable events on the stage, heroes in the throes of love, singing as they struggle and die (Letters of 1786). About this time he set Kayser to work on the music of *Egmont*, and wrote for him an opera the subject of which was taken from the recent story of Cagliostro, and the affair of the Queen's Necklace. His first sketch for the opera was in Italian.

[185] Based on the old phrase *"saltare comoediam,"* literally, to "leap," comedy, an expression dating from the lines when comedians were jesters (*saltatores*) and jumped rather than walked.

[186] One cannot over-emphasize the importance which Goethe invariably attached to moral qualities in the artists whose friendship he sought or accepted, though this has always been denied by his critics. He persisted in this attitude in spite of the artistic loss which it involved. There was no question of a reasoned choice in the matter; it was a vital instinct.

[187] Kayser produced in 1777 a collection of *Lieder* (*Gesänge mit Begleitung des Klaviers*), and Goethe also had his friend's *Lieder* published in several volumes. Bode reproduces some examples in his book on Goethe and music. These *Lieder* display a certain lightness of touch, and their expression is apt and simple. The score of *Scherz, List, und Rache* is kept at the Goethe National Museum at Weimar. Ferdinand Hiller and Max Friedlaender have spoken favourably of it.

[188] At the end of 1789 another project of his, the result of this same devotion to Gluck, which Reichardt shared with him, was a tragedy set to music with choruses in the old classical style, *Die Danaiden*. Goethe was working on this idea during the following ten years.

[189] We already find in the production of his *Proserpina*, in 1815, the three Norns, the three Parcæ (comp. Genast, p. 134).

[190] During the first period of his direction of the Weimar theatre

he got Reichardt to write the music for his ballad operas *Erwin, Claudine,* and *Jery.* He had his *Cagliostro* played as a comedy in 1791 under the title of *Der Grosskophta*; he would have made an opera of it had not he lost all hope of seeing it put on the stage. We may add that he had converted his theatre at Weimar into a little model stage for operetta, and produced the Italian *intermezzi* (short musical plays). He brought with him from Italy the text of twenty-three *opere buffe* by Cimarosa, Anfossi, and others, and translated several of them.

[191] All the fault seems to have been Schiller's; he was quick-tempered and very easily upset. He persuaded Goethe into an insulting attack on Reichardt in *Die Xenien.* Reichardt never lost his fine dignity, never for a moment considered that these affronts released him from the obligations of faithful service which he owed to the genius and the person of Goethe.

[192] In 1820 again Goethe wrote to Zelter, "I feel at once the identity of your compositions with my *Lieder.* The music is simply a lifting force, like the gas in a balloon. With other composers I have always to examine the music to see what view they have taken of the *Lied* and how they have dealt with it."

To know Zelter's *Lieder* is therefore a matter which should interest us deeply: through them we may realize exactly the feelings of Goethe. For this reason I advise the reading of the fine *Lied* of the Harpist in *Wilhelm Meister, "Wer sich der Einsamkeit ergiebt."* It is a model of noble, simple and manly emotion.

[193] There are few stories more moving than the passing, almost at the same time, of the two friends. Goethe died on March 22nd. Zelter, who had written him yet another letter on that very day, lost in a moment *all* his powers and joy of life. He aged ten years in a single day. With trembling lips he said, "I have lost my dearest friend on earth" (*"Ich habe mein Liebstes auf Erden verloren"*). Again he said, "I am like a widow who has lost her man, her lord, the provider of her substance." Early in May he felt seriously ill. Going to his bedroom, he bowed his head gravely before Goethe's

bust, and said, "Your Excellency naturally took precedence of me, but now I follow you" (*"Excellenz halten natürlich den Vortritt, aber ich folge bald nach"*). He took to his bed, and died on May 15th. Who shall say now that Goethe could not love and inspire love?

[194] The collection of Goethe's *Lieder*, composed by Zelter, was published in 1810-12 under the title *Sämtliche Lieder, Balladen, und Romanzen* in four volumes. Reichardt preceded Zelter with his collection of Goethe's *Lieder* in four parts (1809).

[195] Prince Radziwill had been working at it since 1810. His *Faust*, fragments of which Goethe heard in 1811, was given in part (two big scenes) in May, 1819, before the court in a Berlin palace; a prince played Mephisto. The score was published in 1834-35 and the opera was performed over a period of twenty years. Reichardt's collection of Goethe's *Lieder* (1809) included, among some remarkable *Deklamationsstücke*, a fragment of *Faust*, part of the dialogue between Faust and Marguerite in the garden.

Even quicker was Bettina, who, as early as January, 1808, was "drinking in" the *Faust* compositions. She wrote Marguerite's prayer, *"Ach neige, du Schmerzensreiche."*

[196] Fourteen years later (1828-29) Eberwein, at long last, understood. To celebrate Goethe's eightieth birthday he arranged a performance of a *Faust* with music; this was given from time to time up to 1870, and later. Bode quotes several fragments in his second volume, pp. 294-307. They have no great value.

[197] It is to be observed that he had just declined to write a *Samson* for Zelter. It was a wrathful refusal. He had no use, he said, for Jews on the stage, particularly for Samson with "the overwhelming and bestial passion of an immensely powerful God-gifted hero for the most accursed woman's flesh that the earth ever knew" (*"die ganz bestialische Leidenschaft eines überkräftigen, gottbegabten Helden zu dem verfluchtesten Luder das die Erde trägt"*). He knew nothing at that time of Handel's masterly picture of the sorceress.

[198] There were two other projects of the same period—a fragment of dialogue with chorus, *Der Löwenstuhl* (1814), which has a romantic colouring, and a Persian subject which the atmosphere of the *Divan* suggested to him, *Feradeddin and Kolaila* (1816).

[199] I have already noted that from October, 1808, Beethoven was making a vain search for some one to adapt *Faust* for the stage.

[200] When his faithful comedian, Genast, took leave of him shortly before Goethe himself was compelled to resign, the latter sent him these two lines written on a drawing:

"Zur Erinnrung trüber Tage
Voll Bemühen, voller Plage"

("In memory of troublous days, days of sorrow, days of anguish.")

[201] January 29, 1827.

Eckermann seems to have found it odd that a piece "should begin as a tragedy and finish as an opera." Goethe replied: "Yes, it is so. But such is my will."

[202] N.B. He was eighty years old (1829).

[203] Here we must recall the remarkable spectacle of the aged dreamer as he appeared, ten days before his death, to Bettina's young son, "He now seems to belong to another world rather than to this; what passes here below is utterly lost to him in the visions of his imagination." (See my essay on Bettina in this book.)

[204] Many musicians have tried their hand. But not one, not even Schumann, who attempted the final scene in *Faust* (in heaven), had the twofold genius of north and south upon which Goethe insisted and which he himself possessed.

[205] *Lehrjahre*, IV. 2.

[206] I might have added "choruses." One of the questions which occupied him most was that of the chorus in tragedy. The chorus in Greek tragedy had a powerful attraction for him as it had in the compositions of Handel and Gluck, who seemed to him, rightly as we think, the heirs of the great choral art of antiquity. He experimented with various possibilities in his poems set to music,

and especially in the second *Faust*. The main problem was the practical realization, upon the stage, of these ideas. *The Bride of Messina*, at the Weimar Theatre, opened a field of experiment. Schiller had been content with the chorus in unison. The effect was pitiful; it was uninspired and confusing. Goethe, in the third act, divided the singers into two choruses, and used solos, duets, trios, and alternating choruses, with *crescendos* and *decrescendos*, with due regard to the registers of the different voices. (In the memoirs of Genast will be found some notes on his ingenious arrangements.)

207 "*Musik war sie zu nennen*", said Genast of the form of declamation on which he insisted. ("His declamation could have been described as music.")

208 He was accused of "playing chess with his actors."

209 To all who are interested in the theatre I commend the recollections of Genast, "*Aus Weimars klassischer und nachklassischer Zeit. Erinnerungen eines alten Schauspielers.*"

210 I have already emphasized the difference in this matter between Goethe and Schiller. The latter was too fond of speech to music—that is, "melodrama." Goethe proclaimed the musical independence of the spoken word in poetry; with him this is an independent form of music with an existence of its own; it possesses within itself both orchestra and song.

211 Goethe's declamation of poetry was in fact remarkable for light and shade. Pastor Ewald von Offenbach wrote in 1799: "He could express anything he wished without raising or lowering his pitch beyond a few tones. This declamation was graded in infinitely small intervals. Between C and D it would have been possible to distinguish perhaps as many as sixteen fractional tones which could not have been expressed in musical notation. The declamation was characterized by the attack or entry, the melody, the transition into another melody, and the return to the tone on which it had begun." This sounds like a description of the first movement of a sonata of the time.

But with age he lost this art or sacrificed it voluntarily to the "delight in sonority" (*seine Freude am Klange*). When he recited he was too fond of letting his fine bass voice resound and his production was "over-emphasized." This often met with criticism. He was better liked in his reading of comic passages, and Genast avers —who could have imagined it?—that he made an inimitable Falstaff. However, in conversation he always maintained a "soft and measured tone" (*leise und gemessen*). But he had too much vigour and force, not to say brutality, in his make-up. His expression and his acting were at times so violent that at a rehearsal of *King John* the little actress who played opposite him—fainted (Genast).

212 Music in Goethe's poetry is a subject so vast and so profound that a whole book might be devoted to it. Perhaps some day I shall return to the matter. H. Abert in his little book has given it a short but effective chapter, "*Das Musikalische in Goethes Lyrik.*" He shows how powerful was the influence in this direction which Herder excercised on the young Goethe at Strasbourg and how Goethe's genius forthwith evoked the melody which lay hidden in the heart of his poetic emotion. He calls attention to his free rhythm in verse and in prose (*Werther*), a stream of "infinite melody", as it were; to his passages impregnated with actual music, to his great lyrical monologues in musical drama with their *recitativi accompagnati*, their arias, and their torrential rhythm, as in the *Wanderers Sturmlied, Schwager Kronos*, and *Prometheus*. Then, under Italian influence, Goethe passes from the free recitative to the *arioso*.

Iphigenia marks the pinnacle of the watershed, the point of perfection, where Dionysus, the spirit of impulsive flight, is tamed to harmony by the master hand of Apollo. On the further slope of life's mountain top, music, like a stream, returns to its river bed. The torrent subsides, the stream ripples slowly, restrained by the banks which ordered will and understanding have ordained; until, in the *Wanderjahre*, all that is left is a distant murmur, faintly echoed from the mind which encloses it as with a rampart.

213 To this scrutiny we owe the two important publications of

Rheinhold Steig and Fritz Bergemann: *Bettinas Leben und Briefwechsel mit Goethe*, 1921 and 1927.

[214] But in the family papers sold last year Maximiliana gave the incorrect date 1788 for the birth of Bettina. This mistake of three years, which has been unjustly attributed to Bettina, resulted in her sincere belief that she was nineteen and not twenty-two years old when she first met Goethe. . . . May we say that the probable effect of this illusion was that she was always younger than her age?

[215] *"Mein erstes Lesen deiner Bücher! ich verstand sie nicht."* "My first reading of your books. I didn't understand them" (Letter from Bettina to Goethe).

[216] She has not only sealed, as it were, with the world "child," the correspondence with Goethe which she published, *Briefwechsel Goethes mit einem Kinde.* She used it also in her first letters, *"Euer Kind, Dein Herz und gut Mädchen."* Later, in the course of her spiritual affection for Schleiermacher, she called herself his "child" also, and begged for his fatherly love. In Bettina's soul, in all purity of heart, the idea of a father is always mingled with her greatest loves.

[217] She reminded Goethe of this glorious moment in her letter of July 30, 1808: "When at last I found you—was it a dream?—Yes, as I write it seems a wonderful dream. My head rested upon your shoulder, I slept for a few minutes for the first time after four or five sleepless nights. . . ."

[218] A letter from Clemens Brentano to Achim von Arnim, in July, 1807, gives a most joyous account of the visit. Clemens saw the ring, a fine antique, set with the representation of a woman veiling herself. He had no idea, at that time, of putting a bad construction on his sister's relations with the old poet. He was more inclined to congratulate her. But twenty-five years later Clemens, then an old man himself, and a bigot also, was alarmed at the idea of Bettina publishing to the whole of Europe the story of her *"shamelessness."* Lujo Brentano recently published (*"Der jugendliche und der gealterte Clemens Brentano über Bettina und Goethe."*

Sonderabdruck aus dem Jahrbuch des freien Deutschen Hochstifts. Frankfurt, 1929) the letter of horrified prudery which he wrote June 17, 1834, to his sister, after reading the proofs of the first pages of "Goethe's Letters to a Child." The tone of the letter displays an unconscious hypocrisy which would be disgusting if it were not absurd. He deplores that every man in Europe is to be told that Bettina cannot sit in well-brought up fashion on a sofa, and that, most improperly, she sat on the knees of a man who had not the decency to respect the good name of a poor foolish girl. . . . The monument to Goethe which she is having put up reminds one of the pyramids which cost Rhodopis her honour. What is to happen to her children? Her sons run the risk of insults leading to duels. Her daughters may be depraved as the result of the incident or be led to scorn their mother. . . . This man, righteous to the point of sanctity, imposes on his sister this act of penitence, that she should tear from the volume the shameless page and destroy it. . . . "Through the reading of such pages are worthy souls made to stumble. . . ." And he begged her for the future to send him all the drafts for revision before having them printed.

Bettina replied in trenchant fashion, with a disdainful hauteur but in an affectionate tone. She has nothing to hide. What is there to hide? She acted in all innocence, and it was the happiest hour of her life; everything she has been, everything she has done since, she owes to the ecstasy of that moment, the *"ersten erquickenden paradiesischen Schlaf* (the first, refreshing, heavenly sleep)." . . . What right have others to claim control over her? In all the difficult trials of life they left her alone; she has had no one to depend upon and no one troubled himself about her. Who now gives them the right to assume the rôle of guardians of morality? As for her children, she has no cause for concern. If they were to discover any evil in an affair so simple and innocent, they would not be her children; she would refuse to recognize them. Thank God, she means to preserve them from such bigotry and hypocrisy. And she calls her brother an "old nightcap" (*alte Schlafmütze*).

Clemens, much annoyed, replied in the "style of Chanaan."* He condoled, in hypocritical terms, with his "poor" sister, and managed very cleverly to insert in his letter the most offensive allusions under the cloak of kindness. After having compared her to a naked Phryne, he cruelly reminded her of Arnim, "the noble father whom she had forgotten," and the sorrow which the children must feel. Then came disparaging remarks on Goethe, with whom Germany will now have nothing to do; nobody buys his works, and in fact, "the enthusiasm for him has never been genuine." Then he referred again to "the poor good Arnim" . . . and "that poor, silly, godless Bettina. . . ."

But Bettina refuted vehemently the allusion to her "poverty," which was all too real, and to the "pity" which the bigoted brother offered her, with the poisoned flowers of his eloquence. We see her as she stands, proudly aloof, with her Goethe and her God.

219 "You are my daughter. May my son be a brother to you. . . . I am sure that he loves you."

220 The "thou" made its first timid appearance at the end of the letter of October 6, 1807, to which I have already referred. It is found at the end where the "thou" and the "you" are mixed up in childish fashion: *"Euer Kind, Dein Herz und gut Mädchen, das den Göthe gar zu lieb, allein über alles lieb hat, und sich mit seinem Andenken über alles trösten kann"* ("Your child, thy heart, thy little girl who loves Goethe very, very much, loves him only and loves him above all else and whose memory can console her in everything"). But the "thou" only appears regularly with the letters of December, 1807.

221 We find it for the first time on February 22, 1809.

222 "The day when I left you, with a kiss—it was not the kiss which parted us!—I stayed for a whole hour alone in the next room, the room with the piano, and sat on the floor in a corner. . . . You were there, too, quite near me and you never knew it. . . . I

* TRANSLATOR'S NOTE.—Chanaan, the son of Shem, cursed by Noah.

laughed and cried at the same time. . . ." (beginning of January, 1808).

[223] A month before she had told him of Arnim's love for her. . . . "Poor" Arnim (I find myself writing like her brother Clemens! . . .)

[224] She had Goethe's son with her at Frankfurt in April, 1808, and treated him tenderly.

[225] November 3, 1809.

[226] "I cannot fight against you, dear Bettina. You are the best of all my friends, in what you write, in your acts of kindness, in your gifts, and in the love and delight which you bring me. I cannot, therefore, do otherwise than abandon myself to the joy which is mine, and give you in return all my love, even if I must do so in silence."

[227] She had, however, written to him in March or April (see her letter of July 6th).

[228] And, on October 25th of the same year, "all your dear pages, which reached me one after the other." Not one of them has come down to us.

[229] Auction Catalogue 148. Karl Ernst Henrici, Berlin. (February 27-28, 1929.) No. 42, p. 16.

[230] I am not referring to the other sacrifice, the one which Bettina made. She had intended to incorporate these beautiful reminiscences in a book which she would write. But to her loving heart it seemed only a small gift.

[231] October 18, 1810.

[232] November 4, 1810.

[233] What would Goethe have thought, if he could have looked over Bettina's shoulder as she wrote down her convictions, and if he could have read the draft (probably dating from 1826) in which she compared herself to "a spider weaving her net round Goethe, ensnaring him softly, softly. . . ." "And he will not be able to escape!" (Auction Catalogue 148. K. E. Henrici.)

[234] Letter to Moritz Carrière. March 26, 1849.

[235] In *Goethes Briefwechsel mit einem Kinde* (1835 Edition), and the book of 1927 by Fritz Bergemann which has been quoted (p. 206) there is a drawing of Bettina's suggested monument. It is in the neo-antique style of Thorwaldsen, which Goethe liked—only too much, and its academic grandeur possesses no feature which would appeal to us were it not for a little detail, a very womanly one, which sheds a glow of love on the cold marble: it is the little Psyche, symbolizing Bettina in the monument, who touches with her fingers the strings of the huge lyre of the impassive giant and puts her little bare foot on the bare foot of Goethe.

[236] This was a last profession of faith in individualism: "Let everyone sweep in front of his own door, and the whole city will be clean (*Ein jeder kehre vor seiner Thür—und rein ist jedes Stadtquartier*)."

[237] The young man had been deeply moved by his appearance. "He now seems to belong to another world rather than to this; what passes here below (*das Irdische*) is utterly lost to him in the visions of his imagination."

[238] All the passages which I have quoted from her letters in these essays are taken from the authentic correspondence which has been compared with the originals.

[239] Max Friedlaender published a selection of her compositions as a supplement to *Goethes Briefwechsel mit einem Kinde*, Propyläen Verlag, 1920.

Among the manuscripts sold in 1929 was a *Kompositionsbuch* of about a hundred pages, containing her compositions to *Lieder* by Goethe, Arnim, and Hölderlin, whose genius she was one of the first to recognize. In this book she also wrote some of her thoughts, among others, "On the importance of the pause in music." She had studied counterpoint and fugue. Music holds an important place in her correspondence which would be worth a special study, for Bettina's intuitions, though she groped in the dark, delve deeply at times. At the end of this essay I am giving the translation of a strange letter to Goethe, which is, as it were, a monologue on music.

[240] The Grand Duke of Saxe-Weimar, and the Prince of Würtemberg.

[241] "We do not let flies defile pure gold," he wrote to her.

[242] "The king knows that I share your contempt for the censorship and your aversion to it." Humboldt's letter to Bettina. Auction Catalogue 148. Henrici No. 81.

[243] He was released, became Minister of Finance during the Swabian revolution, and was later again sentenced to death.

[244] In 1848 we find him again as one of the leaders of the new Polish revolution.

[245] Auction Catalogue 148. Henrici No. 16.

[246] It often happened that these men, whose lives she had saved, did not inspire her sympathy at all. One of them was Kinkel. In one of her letters (1849) she expresses her disgust for him in pitiless terms; she speaks of his boastfulness, his presumption, his foolish vanity, and his noisiness. . . . "Truly, I have not done it for his sake! I did it because I had to do it. I did it for my own sake. But as a result, everyone has thrown stones at me" (*Ibid.* No. 111).

[247] *Ibid.* No. 119.

[248] The collection of letters sold included forty-two written to the Hungarian poet Kertbeny. They discuss ardently the struggles for Hungarian independence. Kertbeny sent her, in 1849, a flower plucked just before his execution by a man condemned to death.

[249] Memoirs of Mme. Irène Forbes-Mosse.

[250] Her only personal meeting with King Friedrich William IV appears to have been in April, 1845, a long audience at the Monbijou palace on the subject of her *protégés.*

[251] Comp. Goethe the Musician, p. 126.

[252] The following seems still more incredible. Herklots, a musician well known in northern Germany, in 1798 adapted the melody of the *Marseillaise* to a song in honour of the king of Prussia. I am

indebted to Professor Max Friedlaender for reminding me of this fact which Reichardt mentioned.

[253] Comp. Goethe the musician, p. 126.

[254] It was in 1830 that there appeared in northern Germany a *Liederbuch für deutsche Krieger und deutsches Volk* by the school master Carl Weitershausen, who is careful to observe that in one of the songs of victory the melody of the *Marseillaise* seems to have been borrowed (noted by Max Friedlaender).

[255] See p. 28 of "Goethe and Beethoven" I, and p. 181 of the essay on Bettina.

The letter written to Goethe is dated from Berlin, Christmas, 1810 (pp. 333-334 of *Bettinas Leben und Briefwechsel mit Goethe*, published by Fritz Bergemann, 1927, Insel-Verlag).

It is not without hesitation that I hazard a free translation of this extraordinary monologue; it is as if one witnessed, in the dead watches of the night, the birth of a fevered strain of thought. The German historians and philologists themselves, who have made a study of Bettina's writings, admit their doubt as to the meaning of certain phrases. Fortunately the paraphrase which Bettina made in her *Goethes Briefwechsel mit einem Kinde* in 1835 clears up several passages. Dare I maintain that the meaning of the letter, speaking generally, seems clear to me? The interest which I take in it encourages me to hope that many of my readers who are students of Beethoven will also find it clear. Obscured by the awkward and tentative expressions, there is to be found a lively and profound musical intuition; we may glean from Bettina a better understanding of Beethoven's soul than she herself possessed.

I have placed in brackets the passages taken from Bettina's paraphrase of 1835.

[256] When Bettina uses the word "magic" she means "the outcome of genius."

[257] ["Zelter, among others, will never allow anything to pass which he does not fully understand."]

[258] Comp. Goethe's words to Humboldt, "Music is purely and simply irrational (*die reine Unvernunft*): the written word is concerned with reason and with nothing else."

[259] "*Auf die einzelnen Werkzeuge* (*Menschen*) ("on isolated instruments, that is, men") I interpret this as the rhythmic action and reaction which take place between the genius and the human race, one depending upon the other. Genius must have a substance in which to implant life.

[260] "*Wie das Herz gebaut ist*" ("according to the structure of each heart"). My reading of the paragraph is this. In the ages which are past music submitted to definite intellectual rules. Nowadays the subjectivity of the sentiment reigns supreme and genius is the master. But who can claim that these obscure forces will always be directed to the noblest end?

[261] ["*Zelter muss vermeiden, dem Beethoven gegenüberzustehen.*"] ("Zelter must be careful not to fall foul of Beethoven").

[262] "*Wie ein Holzbock.*"

[263] Literally "*wenn er alles will.*"

[264] "*Wenn er sich nicht loss macht von den Handwerkern.*"

[265] "*Uhrwerk.*" In Bettina's famous letter of July 1810, where she spoke for the first time to Goethe of Beethoven, this is the word which she employs to describe the whole of human effort as opposed to the one man Beethoven, the only untrammelled creator. "Just as the mechanism of a clock (*Uhrwerk*) centres upon an axis, so does every form of human activity centre upon him. He alone of himself brings to birth." . . . Comp. p. 18.

[266] Let us make a *résumé* of this monologue which is charged with Beethoven's feeling, and with revolt against the school of thought which held him in contempt.

Bettina pleads the cause of the irrational in art, and, above all, in music. She sets the genius who expresses freely the forces within him against the cold reasoners, the scholars who employ borrowed formulas. Music, if it would live, must release itself from the mechanical spirit, must discover the freedom of the will, the springs of the vital forces. There is but one road by which it may be reached—meditation, concentration, inspiration. Beethoven has revealed to her the direct path.

We should compare these ideas with those which her visit to Beethoven inspired during the previous spring according to the letters which I quoted early in my first essay. ("Goethe and Beethoven" Chapter I.) It is Beethoven's harvest; he himself was the sower.